Belinda Tato/Jose Luis Vallejo

Networked Urbanism

Design Thinking Initiatives for a Better Urban Life

 **Harvard University
Graduate School of Design**

Networked Urbanism

Networked Urbanism was a series of studios in the Urban Planning and Design Department at the Harvard University Graduate School of Design taught between 2010 and 2014.

The Networked Urbanism studio aimed to bring network-design thinking to the forefront of design disciplines, and strove to solve real-world problems on the ground, providing an alternative to the traditional approach of designing urban environments from a bird's-eye view and a single designer's perspective.

Networked Urbanism not only examined the physical dimension of the city, but also its social processes and fluxes, developing initiatives that generated spontaneous trans-formations and set up conditions for change.

The Networked Urbanism studio pro-vided the framework for students to pursue their own interests, find their own means of expression, and create their own paths. They were encouraged to work with others, to create connections, and to search for new problems and opportunities that underlie our society, visibly or subtly. Overall, they were expected to explore the city and design new tools to creatively improve urban life.

Instructors
Belinda Tato, Jose Luis Vallejo

Students
Kate Balug, Angela Clubb, Jennifer Corlett, Krystelle Denis, Irene Figueroa, Natalia Gaerlan, Jeffrey Goodman, Karyssa K. Halstead, Chen Huang, Christopher Johnson, Melissa A. Jones, Andrew P. Leonard, Lulu Li, Scott Liang, Hung Kai Liao, Joe Chun Zu Liao, Kevin J. Madden, Thomas McCourt, Jennifer Mills, Stacy Dee Morton, Kelly Murphy, Kathleen Onufer, James W. Perakis, Robert Pietrusko, Victoria Pineros, Claire V. Ricker, Khyati Saraf, Benjamin Scheerbarth, Jack Schonewolf, Lydia Scott, Soomin Shin, Mike Styczynski, Matthew Swaidan, Molly Turner, Josh Westerhold, Jean You, Hansley Yuñez, Ziyi Zhang

Final Review Critics
Angélica Allende Bris, Ramiro Almeida, Kenny Bailey, Kate Balug, Alan Berger, Paul B. Bottino, Angelyn Chandler, Carol Coletta, Felipe Correa, Daniel D'Oca, Leslie Davol, Benjamin de la Pena, Gareth Doherty, Jacqueline Douglas, Gines Garrido, Theaster Gates, Ole Goethe, Jeff Goldenson, Michael Hooper, Nigel Jacob, Blair Kamin, Olympia Kazi, Matthew Kiefer, Roland Krebs, Alexandra Lange, Jim Lasko, Max Liboiron, Helen Lochhead, Yanni Loukissas, Ann Lusk, Randi Mail, Helen Marriage, Catherine McMahon, Selene Mota, Georgia Murray, Aaron Naparstek, Liz Nunn, Philipp Oswalt, Dimitris Papanikolaou, Robert Pietrusko, Lynn Richards, Jeff Risom, David Sanderson, Nitin Sawhney, Jeffrey Schnapp, Jose Selgas, Renata Sentkiewicz, Jesse Shapins, James Solomon, Pete Stidman, James Stockard, Bill Traynor, Deanna Van Buren, Anthony Vanky, Ed Walker, Enrique Walker, Christopher Winship

#networkedurbanism

Belinda Tato and Jose Luis Vallejo

Urbanism is the mirror in which the many aspects and layers of society are reflected. Cities were first developed to support basic human activities, but have gradually transformed into complex, evolving, living laboratories, where socio-environmental relations are constantly being redefined. In this context, and with over half of the world's population now living in urban areas, it has become clear that there can be no single solution to environmental, social, or economic challenges.

Moreover, it is necessary to work on a variety of aspects of city life simultaneously. The multilayered contemporary experience demands a more holistic approach to designing cities. The existing model focuses on the static layer of the physical environment (infrastructures, buildings, materials, geometries, etc.) and its economic aspects, while ignoring the social dimensions. This has led to the creation of a dominant discipline that oversimplifies and reduces the complexity of urban ecosystems. A new paradigm should recognize, nurture, and celebrate the dynamism of urban life—its processes, relationships, patterns, links, and interactions.

At the same time, the Internet is the "space" where the most successful models of collective creation and self-organization are being tested. Real-time connectivity, ubiquity, and unlimited access to large flows of information and knowledge have fundamentally altered the way we relate to and work with each other. The digital realm allows and promotes interaction between people, while physical space is increasingly more controlled and restricted, becoming progressively less spontaneous and creative.

The Web has boosted the social identities and collective interests of people, who are becoming a force with considerable influence in politics, social issues, and urban life. Citizens have evolved from consumers to prosumers, producing ideas, knowledge, information, and content, and becoming key players in an interwoven and augmented reality. We cannot address the design and transformation of cities without considering the potential of digital technologies, and understanding how they can enhance urban complexity, creating healthier, richer, more diverse, and more connected environments.

This is the new context in which designers operate today, and new contexts require new ways of working. In today's connected world, urban design can no longer be addressed from a singular perspective, but should result from an open and collaborative network of creative professionals, technical experts, citizens, and other stakeholders. As disciplinary boundaries are blurring, we need to explore the new role of the designer as an activator, mediator, and curator of social processes in a networked reality. Above all, we must develop and test tools that allow citizens to be active participants at all stages: before, during, and after the design process.

Designers need to pay attention to the multiple forces at play in the construction of the territory and its institutions, as well as the redefinition of the operational processes of architecture, landscape, and urban design practice and research. It is necessary to be aware of our socio-environmental responsibility and promote emergent collaborative forms of government, linking municipal thinking, urban policy, education, and civic engagement.

Networked Urbanism promotes the exploration of new tools that can become the catalyst to spark creativity and multiply the possibilities of interaction and connection among individuals in the search for more healthy and sustainable communities. The studio blends critical theory with hands-on practice, social innovation with urban entrepreneurship, and progressive thinking with community engagement. The studio challenges future designers to develop initiatives that reconcile existing physical conditions with the emerging needs of citizens through network-design thinking, and promotes active participation in the redefinition of the contemporary city.

Digitas Meets Humanitas: The Projects of Networked Urbanism

Blair Kamin

There was no Internet in 1938 when the eminent Chicago sociologist Louis Wirth wrote his classic essay, "Urbanism as a Way of Life." Taking note of the phenomenal growth of such industrial cities as New York and Chicago, as well as the lack of an adequate sociological definition of urban life, Wirth articulated parameters of enduring relevance.

Cities should not be defined by the quantity of their land mass or the size of their population, he wrote. Rather, they were best understood by pinpointing their distinctive qualities: "a relatively large, dense, and permanent settlement of socially heterogeneous individuals."[1] That heterogeneity, Wirth observed, had the effect of breaking down the rigid social barriers associated with small-town and rural life. It increased both mobility and instability, causing individuals to join organized groups to secure their identity amid the city's ceaseless flux. "It is largely through the activities of the voluntary groups," Wirth observed, "that the urbanite expresses and develops his personality, acquires status, and is able to carry on the round of activities that constitute his life-career."[2]

Implicit in his analysis was the notion that these networks would be formed through the technologies of their time: by letter, by telephone, by telegraph, by the newspaper, and, of course, by face-to-face contact. Amid today's ongoing digital revolution, that part of Wirth's otherwise prescient analysis seems antique.

In that sense, nothing has changed and everything has changed since the publication of "Urbanism as a Way of Life" more than 75 years ago. Half of the world's population lives in urban areas; that share, the United Nations predicts, will rise to roughly two-thirds by 2050. As in Wirth's time, urbanization has spawned acute problems, from China's acrid skies to India's vast slums. Yet while urbanites still ally themselves with groups, the means by which they do this has shifted entirely. Think of the recent spate of "Facebook revolutions." Human communication is now overwhelmingly digital, and digital urbanism has become a pervasive part of city life, whether it takes the form of sensors embedded in highways or apps that let us know when the bus is coming.

The question is whether we are fully realizing the potential of these tools to improve the quality of the built environment and, with it, the quality of urban life. In short, can the virtual enrich the physical?

Madrid architects Belinda Tato and Jose Luis Vallejo, principals of the firm Ecosistema Urbano, believe in the value of this link and have set out to prove its worth through their practice and their Harvard University Graduate School of Design studio, Networked Urbanism.

as parochial. The architects subscribe to the philosophy of "going glocal." As they have written, "every urban project is born in a constant movement between the direct experience and specificity of the local context, and the global, shared flow of information and knowledge."[4]

One of the "glocal" issues American cities face is the rapid expansion of bicycles as a mode of transportation—a stark contrast to China, where members of the new middle class abandon bikes for the status symbol of a car and, in the

The architects belong to a new generation that decries the self-referential "object buildings" enabled by digital design. Yet like Frank Lloyd Wright, who viewed the machine as an agent of progressive social and aesthetic change, they see the computer as a friend, not an enemy.

This perspective has helped them realize such socially-conscious projects as the Ecopolis Plaza in Madrid, which transformed an old industrial site into a child care and recreation center that is as visually striking as it is ecologically sensitive. Tato and Vallejo have imparted this creative approach to their students and the students have run with it, as the impressive results collected in this book show.

The first thing that distinguishes Tato and Vallejo's pedagogy is its starting points, which are unapologetically practical and local—an anomaly within the theory-driven, globally-focused world of academic architectural culture. Instead of parachuting into some far-flung locale, their students engage the place where they live: greater Boston. This affords the students time for repeat visits to their project sites and a deeper understanding of people and their needs than can be gleaned on a lightning-fast overseas tour. But it would be inaccurate to characterize the process and product of Networked Urbanism

process, worsen traffic congestion and air pollution. But the growth of urban cycling has brought a dramatic increase in bicycle thefts. The vast majority of these thefts go unreported to police because the stolen bikes are rarely found. The victims feel powerless. Harvard student Lulu Li used to be one of them. She's had her bike stolen twice, once from the racks in front of the GSD. "When I started talking to friends about it, I quickly realized that most everyone has had some sort of bike theft experience," she said in an interview with Harvard's Office of Sustainability.

Li's response was to design a successful online platform, Bikenapped, which maps where bike thefts occur. The website allows bike theft victims to avoid these trouble spots, share their stories, and perhaps even prevent future thefts. The interactivity afforded by digital technology is crucial to the enterprise, as one posting from August 2013 shows: "Flexible Kryptonite lock was cut between 4:30–6:20 p.m. at the bike rack outside Fenway movie theatre," a victim named Deborah wrote about the loss of her white Vita bike with small black fenders, a white seat and a value of $550. "Busy intersection, loads of people. No one saw anything. Cameras point at doors, not bike rack." The theater's owners are now on notice that they should reposition one of their cameras. More important, Li has drawn upon her individual experience to frame a collective digital response, one that was technologically impossible when Wirth penned "Urbanism as a Way of Life."

The students in Networked Urbanism have taken on other pressing problems of our time, such as the need for recycling that helps protect the environment. But waste doesn't happen by chance; it's a result of bad design.

Consider what two students came up with

Yet such a myopic world view privileges a formalist approach to architecture at the expense of the field's rich social promise. Architecture isn't a large-scale version of sculpture. It shapes the world in which we live.

The genius of Networked Urbanism is that it isn't teaching students to be geniuses. It's teaching them to be creative problem solvers, builders of smart digital networks, and thus, builders of smarter urban communities. That's a brighter, more responsible vision of

as they analyzed the very Bostonian problem of discarded oyster shells. The students, Jenny Corlett and Kelly Murphy, devised a way to break the cycle of restaurants mindlessly throwing out used oyster shells, which, in turn, wind up in landfills. Their solution: collect and dry the shells, then use them to help grow new oysters and rebuild oyster reefs in Boston Harbor.

The plan would have a disproportionate impact because oysters affect many other species in their ecosystem. They improve water quality by removing algae, plankton, and pollutants from the water. And the oyster reefs provide a habitat for small species like snails and shrimp, thereby increasing a region's biodiversity. It's hard to argue with projected outcomes like that—or with Corlett and Murphy's marketing skills: before their final presentation, they served their visiting critics oysters on the half shell.

Those who believe that architecture schools exist solely to teach students to be heroic designers might smirk at such examples. Recently, the dean of a prestigious American architecture school provocatively argued that the problem of people complaining about object buildings is that people are complaining about object buildings. Making memorable objects, this dean said, is the core of what architects and architecture are about.

the future than the dumbed-down version of digital urbanism you see on sidewalks today—people staring at their smartphones, lost in their own private worlds. In contrast, the projects of Networked Urbanism offer a new, intelligent way to form and vitalize the social networks that Wirth identified as crucial to the continued well-being of urban life. Together, these designs confer fresh relevance upon the sociologist's ringing declaration that "metropolitan civilization is without question the best civilization that human beings have ever devised."[3]

1   Louis Wirth, "Urbanism as a Way of Life," *American Journal of Sociology* 44, no. 1 (July 1938): 8.

2   Ibid., 23.

3   Ecosistema Urbano, "About," http://ecosistemaurbano.com/portfolio/about/.

4   Louis Wirth, "The City (The City as a Symbol of Civilization)," *The Papers of Louis Wirth*, the Joseph Regenstein Library, Special Collections, University of Chicago, box: 39, folder: 6.

A Different
Design Education

Lulu Li

When I met Belinda Tato and Jose Luis Vallejo for the first time, during the initial session of the Networked Urbanism studio in the fall of 2012, I was unnerved by the openness of the brief they laid out for us. "Do anything you want," they said, "but you really have to do it."

We were asked to take an idea beyond a proposal in the controlled environment of a classroom to an actualized reality, big or small, that affects our city. And we had to test our ideas in the "real world," if only to invalidate them. I was in unfamiliar territory.

motivating in its guidance and encouragement.

But beyond the projects themselves, the studio fostered something even more significant: a new willingness to push one's own boundaries, and the confidence to really implement an idea.

Oftentimes, we are intimidated by the perceived lack in our own knowledge and abilities as young designers. Yet the studio encouraged us to make mistakes, to test ourselves, and of course, to learn new things. From collaborating with police departments and cycling advocates,

Having recently had my bike stolen, I settled on the issue of bike theft. For someone accustomed to the traditional studio environment, bringing my bike project beyond the walls of Gund Hall proved to be intimidating at first. I quickly learned that the rules of the studio were irrelevant when dealing with issues in a real-world context. My assumptions were constantly brought into question; my progress was dependent on the cooperation of parties with different agendas; my own understanding of the project was continuously evolving with each new development. Though difficult at times, the process was rewarding as the project grew to have a life of its own, from an internally driven idea to an effort of collaboration and engagement.

To bring a proposal from the hypothetical playground of the studio to the unpredictable complexity of the real world was a humbling experience. In the controlled studio environment, proposals are built upon untested frameworks. There is little if no feedback loop between the project and the context in which it is meant to operate. Many times, this is not the interest of an academic studio. Yet when these ideas are brought into context, we learn that sometimes the problems we imagine belie the real issues at play. Our "solutions" are built on mistaken assumptions, and the real effort of making something happen depends much more on the cooperation of others than on our own will. This feedback loop is a particularly powerful learning mechanism, humbling in its revelation of my own naiveté and

to developing websites and media campaigns, I learned skills that are not typical of a design school education but are increasingly relevant to designers today.

Enabled by technology and facilitated by communication media, it is now easier than ever to contribute our voices to the discussion of how cities operate. Networked Urbanism is very much a studio of our times, a call to action, an invitation to join in the discussion beyond the doors of the classroom. We were asked to contribute, with an open mind, what we have learned to the spaces we live in, the communities we are a part of, and the issues we find important.

At the end of the semester, the final review was less a critique of the projects than a showcase for the work we had accomplished at that point. The projects were not for the invited critics to validate. The most important critics—the people who believed in our ideas, who shared them, supported them, helped us make them into reality—had already given the necessary feedback. Though the project began in the studio, it had moved beyond the limits of the classroom to have agency and relevance of its own. Two years later, Bikenapped.com still receives regular traffic, producing maps of bike thefts in Boston and San Francisco through community submissions.

The invaluable lessons of this experience continue to stay with me.

Out of the Studio, Onto the Streets

Scott Liang, Thomas McCourt, Benjamin Scheerbarth

Our experience with the Networked Urbanism studio began with a feeling of uncertainty and excitement. The course description was vague yet intriguing, and before our colleagues in other studios had even moved into their desks, we were already tasked with our first assignments. In just the first two weeks, we would deliver three high-quality short films in addition to a number of other projects that gave us great latitude to explore the topic of the studio, share an introspective film about ourselves, and

any status-quo approach from dominating. The diversity of backgrounds and talents in our studio was put on display: architects and computer programmers, planners and economists, landscape urbanists and lawyers. Each contributed a unique perspective and working style to the studio. The three of us that formed Team Place Pixel gravitated toward each other based on a mutual admiration and the potential for synergy we had seen in the work produced in the previous exercises. Scott had set himself apart

experience working under tight deadlines with students from disciplines other than our own. The rapid production schedule at the beginning of the semester set a somewhat dizzying pace, but the reasons behind it soon became clear.

By the end of the semester, at the time of the studio's final review, we knew we were ready. We went into our final presentation, in front of a jury of esteemed critics and practitioners, confident and proud of the work we had done. Not long before, we had presented our project to audiences at MIT, and as winning entrants to a competition at ABX2013, New England's largest architecture exposition. We had also built a network of more than 20 advisors and supporters from academia and both the public and private sector. In retrospect, we had created the foundation for what has since become a full-time startup company: Place Pixel.

What happened in between, from the start of the semester to the final review, is the fondest memory of our time at the Graduate School of Design and an experience that we will never forget.

The studio topic of "waste" served as a guide, a placeholder, a common focus to facilitate the introspective exercises that helped us situate ourselves and to see how we each thought through complex problems. The one rule that was strictly adhered to throughout the first several exercises was that no group could be comprised of individuals who were from the same program, or who had worked together before. This forced us each out of our comfort zones, introduced new frictions, and prevented

as a talented designer with grand ambitions; Ben had established himself as a dreamer with a philosophical approach toward societal problems; TJ brought a sharp logical edge and a knack for distilling complex ideas into clear communication. On paper we shared almost nothing in common, but Jose and Belinda saw something intangible in our potential to work as a unit and encouraged us to team up together.

The multidisciplinary background of our group proved to be our greatest asset. We developed hybrid working styles that capitalized on the traits each of us contributed to the team: a source of energy to keep the gears turning when the project began to stall, a charismatic speaker to form connections and relationships, a natural organizer to juggle all of the time commitments, an abstract thinker to push the boundaries of our concept, a rational thinker to keep us focused on implementation. There was not one among us who could be each of these things, but together we were all of them.

Our instructors had the highest of hopes for us, and knew all too well how easily a project can stall if momentum is not maintained and benchmarks are not achieved. They allowed us the autonomy to set our own goals and the freedom to explore tangents that might help us to transform our initial approach, but also knew the exact moments to reign us in and help us to reestablish focus on concrete objectives.

At times it was stressful, at times exasperating, but always it helped us to achieve more than we thought we could. The oscillation between sandbox-style freedom and firm

one-on-one critiques made this studio a true graduate-school experience. The absence of presentation templates, prescribed processes, and uniform guidance in general allowed us to take ownership of the project. And ownership, for us, was the single greatest motivational factor, pushing us to devote more energy than we ever could have individually, or ever would have imagined we could before the studio began.

The constraints placed on our creative process were minimal. We were encouraged to pursue as many different avenues of inquiry as we could manage, and allowed to deviate from the predefined objectives of the studio if it would ultimately push our project forward. In spite of all the openness and flexibility inherent in the process, one requirement was inviolable: it was unacceptable for this project to exist only within the studio. What we were creating was to become a workable design solution to a real-world problem. We were taught that some of the most essential forces that drive implementation are networking, outreach, and publicity. It was only with an invested network of stakeholders that a project like ours could begin to generate the momentum necessary to endure beyond the end of the semester. Without a certain level of refinement and presence outside of the classroom, this project would have remained little more than a creative idea—a set of drawings, diagrams, and studio presentations we might remember fondly, but which would never see the light of day.

To this end, within a week of forming our team we were building a network of advisors. Beginning with familiar faculty from the GSD, we soon broadened our network to include experts and researchers in various related disciplines from nearby schools such as Northeastern and MIT, professional practitioners from city planning offices and entrepreneurial incubators, and people grappling with the same problems we were from as far away as Austria and Australia.

This network helped us to not only situate ourselves at the cutting edge of the academic discourse in this area, but also exposed us to a number of opportunities to present our ideas to the public. This exposure caught the attention of several officials from city governments including Boston and Philadelphia, and proved to be deeply inspirational for us on a personal level. We found ourselves presenting to audiences of discerning professionals and skeptical researchers, and came away from the experience knowing that our ideas had traction and real-world merit. It was at once humbling and exhilarating to display our work side-by-side with representative projects from established design firms. It takes a unique mindset and plenty of confidence for a professor to allow a number of nascent projects to go out on the streets, to make bold claims, and to take on seemingly insurmountable challenges.

At times it is a struggle, but it is only through confronting those challenges that these projects can grow beyond the classroom and begin to make a real difference in the world. The safer choice, to be sure, would be to nurture speculative projects that exist solely through their representation on paper, graphic boards, and miniature models. In the Networked Urbanism studio, however, confining ourselves to these academic artifacts would have been tantamount to failure.

We learned what it means to truly devote yourself to a project, not just in terms of hours spent working, but in terms of the amount of yourself you invest in it. Because we were pushing to achieve something real, to actually implement a design solution that we had conceived, we went above and beyond anything we had put into a studio course before or since. There is nothing more fulfilling than to see something you care deeply about come to life, and that is something we were able to experience. It is for this reason that we look back and are grateful for the guidance, the inspiration, and—most importantly—the trust that we received along the way.

After the semester ended, we applied for and were accepted into the Harvard Innovation Lab, an entrepreneurship incubator funded by the university. There, we continued to work on expanding our network, generating publicity, and pursuing investments from venture capital firms who believed in the demonstrated potential of our idea. As of our graduation from the GSD, we will be working full time on Place Pixel, and the startup company we have formed around the project has expanded to include two full-time software developers. We could not be more excited about where this will lead, living the dream of working for ourselves on a labor of love.

Scott Liang, Thomas McCourt, Benjamin Scheerbarth

The Real Learning Begins When Things Go Live

A conversation with
Paul B. Bottino

Paul B. Bottino is cofounder and executive director of TECH, Technology and Entrepreneurship Center at Harvard.

"TECH's mission is to advance the understanding and practice of innovation and entrepreneurship through experiential education: by initiating, advancing and informing student projects. TECH helps faculty create and deliver innovation and entrepreneurship project courses, provides students with project support, and sponsors and advises student groups working to build the Harvard innovation community. TECH is based on the belief that boundaries— between disciplines, people, organizations, and ideas—need to be crossed continually to create the insights that lead to innovations because socially useful and commercially viable advancements require the right mix of scientific and engineering knowledge, entrepreneurial know-how, and worldly perspective."[1]

Belinda Tato & Jose Luis Vallejo TECH promotes experiential education, a pedagogical approach that informs many methodologies in which educators purposefully engage with learners in direct experience and focused reflection in order to increase their knowledge, develop their skills, clarify their values, and develop their capacity to contribute to their communities. The Networked Urbanism studio incorporates this methodology, requiring participants to leave their comfort zone in order to introduce them to realities in today's society—outside the walls of academia—in which designer's skills are needed.

Do you think that this non-academic, feedback-driven process should be used more often in design courses? Does it help to foster an entrepreneurial spirit among students?

Paul B. Bottino Absolutely. Though it is only non-academic in the sense of that word that means concerned solely with matters of theoretical importance. I consider it academic because it is central to learning, which is my chosen sense of the word. The kind of experiential education that my students and I practice does have practical ends as well as theoretical. But in a creative economy, where knowledge is the primary means of production, education is inextricably linked to practical ends. All of the educators and learners I know—be they at the lifelong, higher, secondary, elementary, or natural level—want to create useful knowledge for their desired ends, and those ends include everything imaginable on the spectrum of human experience. In my case, and I believe this is true of the Networked Urbanism studio, the end goal is to help build students' innovative capacity. In order to do that, educators and students must jointly go on an implicit knowledge exploration. It is obvious but worth saying that knowledge about the future and the new designs that will inhabit it is not explicit, meaning you can't enter search terms in Google and get answers, even if Google had access to every bit of knowledge available. Instead, it is a research process in which you craft a probe in the form of a design concept and take it to people to educe knowledge about it. If it is a new concept, which it must be to qualify as a potential innovation, then it is going to generate new thoughts. The designer takes those new thoughts not as answers, but rather as feedback. The endeavor of the designer is to transform concepts into value. Value is a utility function; it derives from the use of designs by some number of people. So the essential way designers create value is by engaging in a process of formulation-feedback-reformulation that transforms neurons firing into words, visuals, prototypes, and designs. In my experience, learning via this process is the only way to develop the kind of embodied knowledge that lasts and evolves. Willingly engaging in this full experience and being vulnerable to it is the essence of the entrepreneurial spirit. And, as Oliver Wendell Holmes, said, "A mind that is stretched by a new experience can never go back to its old dimensions."

is given or known, from innovating, where it is not. Yet we should still call creative solutions that are widely used "innovations." To this way of thinking, the full experience of innovating starts with some kind of finding — finding problems people don't know they have or finding opportunities others don't see. These kinds of findings emerge from change. Change causes uncertainty about the meaning of existing things and whether they are still useful and valuable.

BT & JLV Networked Urbanism encourages students to choose a topic at the intersection of their interests and society's needs. They have to take the initiative and make decisions. Projects become unique and linked to their personal stories, many of them living beyond the term.This isn't the traditional academic approach but it is a common entrepreneurial construct, and designers are increasingly expected to define both the problem and the solution.

Do you think that "problem finding" skills have become a fundamental base for innovation?

PB Yes, most certainly. I would say those skills have always been essential to innovation, but it is probably more apt to call them something else because in many cases you don't need to find the problem, it is in clear view. Consider certain diseases where the problems are well known — when a treatment or cure is discovered, invented, and developed, it is very likely immediately deemed an innovation. This is a process of innovation that occurs almost entirely by devising a new solution to an existing problem. I think it is fair to differentiate creative problem-solving, where the problem

The designer interprets change, sees things differently, and creates new meaning and value. Because there is so much change, the possibilities are endless so it is essential to filter them through one's values, interests, and capabilities to make a starting choice. This is wonderful for the educational experience because it supplies personal purpose, relevance, and intrinsic motivation to the exploration.

BT & JLV One of the crucial benefits during the Networked Urbanism studio has been the cross-pollination of students with many different backgrounds from all the programs within the GSD. Moreover, the collaboration with people outside of the studio enhanced the innovation of the projects exponentially, since students are required to build up connections with others, creating a network of advisors and professionals within the field, as well as existing and potential community members.

Is transdisciplinary collaboration now a necessary ingredient for successful entrepreneurship and innovation?

PB It is probably too much to say that it is absolutely necessary in all cases because

there will always be instances of people seeing things differently and innovating without too much assistance, but it feels like those are edge cases that are more and more rare. More the norm is where the challenge is complex, and seeing and approaching things differently comes from a combination of perspectives and abilities. It is often hard for one person to see things differently. Some people are more agile than others at changing frames internally; most need collaboration and other inputs to do it. I think this is due to a combination of the way our neural pathways are formed and maintained and a lack of meta-thinking practice. That combined with increasingly specialized knowledge domains and the training and concentration necessary to master those domains means that collaborating with people from other areas, worldviews, and walks of life increases your chances of seeing things differently, getting the diversity of feedback you need and finding the knowledge resources you need to create value.

BT & JLV The learning experience includes the possibility to learn from consequences, mistakes, and successes. This methodology emphasizes the value of the process itself, in contrast to a teaching approach primarily focused on the end results.

How would you value the process versus the end results? Can we introduce failure/uncertainty as part of the development of the learning process?

PB You are being charitable because we people have proven ourselves to be pointless predictors! And our ever-growing connectedness and complexity are going to give computer power and big data analytics a long battle before we get much better. So as far as I can see, the value is in the process, and the end results are more or less kaleidoscopic: when the twirling stops for an instant, we see a pattern, rationalize how we got there, codify explanations, and issue predictions based on the code. The twirl resumes and reminds us of our folly but we can't give up the game and our illusion of control. My response is to emphasize good practice—valuing process over results—in the hope that more often than not good results will emerge from good practice. Part of any good practice is periodic reflection intended to prolong the period where one is open to discovering the right practice for the right situation. That reflection includes looking at how the failure and uncertainty inherent in the process affects our practice; asking how we respond to and perceive failures; and how we perform and make decisions and communicate in uncertain circumstances.

BT & JLV Think Big and Start Small are two of the 10 guidelines for the course, and are also key concepts for innovation in general.

Do you have any advice about how to fill the gap between the "think" phase and the "start" phase? What are the most common challenges in the transition between the design phase and the actual implementation of the project in the real world?

PB Your eighth guideline for the studio is a great start, "Act Now!" (and ask questions later and along the way). Whenever possible, it's a good idea to transform thoughts and words into actions and to test them with people. It is the formulation of something that people can see, touch, and experience that stimulates the most useful feedback. It is much easier to close this gap with virtual designs than it is with the physical, but you can shrink it with models and simulations. In the virtual cases, the transition isn't a bright line but a continual back and forth—two steps forward, one step back—of testing with people and redesigning until you realize your test subjects have become users and you feel you've made a phase change to implementation. With physical designs and more complicated virtual designs, there are clearer phase distinctions and cut-over moments. The real learning begins when things go live. The greatest challenge I see designers face in these moments is handling the pressure and responding to the unforeseen requirements that are now coming from stakeholders external to the design team, whereas before they were self-imposed. These events stress the entire design organism, from the belief that what you are doing is valuable to the little details that make it work. The best teams use systems thinking and parallel processing to tend to the entire organism in order to be as ready as they can be for these moments.

BT & JLV Historically, design schools have been somewhat segregated from other disciplines, and have been considered to be niche institutions. In the last decade, design

has emerged as an overarching discipline, and design methods (design thinking) are strongly influencing other fields. These methods are frequently adopted by a wide range of disciplines, from scientific to humanistic ones.

How would you explain this opening? Has the role of the designer shifted from designing a building or product to "enhancing society"?

PB Design thinking fits a classic technology innovation paradigm, which is that it takes on the order of 30 years to emerge from inception to widespread adoption. Ideas spread faster now but the 30-year rule still works for big changes. Design thinking is "process know-how" that fits the broad definition of technology. I would trace its origins back to 1961 and the publication of *Synectics* by William J. J. Gordon.[2] So many factors contribute to where it is today but perhaps the two main ones are increasing complexity frustrating a purely analytical approach and the shift from an industrial economy to a knowledge economy where the emphasis moved from labor, equipment, and capital to people, engendering a natural embrace of the human-centered precept of design thinking. The designer's role changed right along with that. With a focus on people, the essential question is not what to make or how to make it, it is why to make it; so inexorably, designers (which includes makers by many other formal names) engage the issue of why, embody it in their designs, and find themselves working at the highest level of value creation.

BT & JLV You work as an educator with students and professionals coming from various institutions, with different backgrounds, education, and expectations. In your experience, do designers and/or students of design have special capabilities for creative problem solving?

PB All children have the basic capabilities and unfortunately it seems mainstream schooling retrains them to concentrate on solving right-answer problems with predetermined tools. Design students seem to have either never lost, or have managed to reawaken, the childhood ability to see things differently, dive into open-ended challenges and try to figure things out without knowing the "right" way. That and a healthy quotient of cultivated empathy and the energy to exercise it regularly is what I see setting design students apart.

BT & JLV Networked Urbanism provides students with a toolbox of 10 guidelines to use during the research process:
1. EXPLORE
2. RESEARCH
3. NETWORK
4. SHARE
5. BE OPEN
6. THINK BIG
7. START SMALL
8. ACT NOW!
9. COMMUNICATE
10. MOVE BEYOND.[3]
Which other ingredients would you add to it?

PB This is a tremendous set to which I'd add:
11. DECLARE your ignorance: embrace what you don't know and can't explain, and cultivate it as an energy source to ward off the tendency to believe you have an answer before you do—and the tendency not to risk losing what you think you have.
12. DEFY known authorities: their dissonance is as good an indication of value as your adopter's resonance.
13. FOCUS on the meaning of your design: value springs from metaphorical shifts.
14. NARRATE the story of your design complete with round characters, rich settings, true heroes, and real villains.

1   Excerpt from TECH website, http://tech.seas. harvard.edu/.
2   William J. J. Gordon, *Synectics: The Development of Creative Capacity* (New York: Harper & Row, 1961).
3   See pages 30–31 for a full description.

Reflection in Action

Belinda Tato and Jose Luis Vallejo

In the context of the digital revolution, contemporary socio-political dynamics call for reflection on the way we teach and learn. Spaces and instruments for learning, methods and hierarchies, places and distances have all been brought into question. Beyond and around learning, there is an ongoing paradigm change that involves almost every aspect of culture and society. The way we address and manage processes, products, and knowledge is evolving, aided by new technological possibilities and critical "meta" reflections: from competition to collaboration and cooperation; from centralization to P2P; from pyramidal structures to grassroots, horizontal networks; from professional secrecy to transparency; from closed R&D to crowdsourcing; from intellectual property restrictions to copyleft and open-source initiatives; from closed designs or services to open roadmaps that embrace perpetual beta.

Regardless of this complex contemporary reality, design education too often still focuses exclusively on the end result, working as though in an isolated bubble, disconnected both from other disciplines and from the real world, disinterested in the constraints and challenges that exist beyond the classroom, which could actually enrich and inform the project for a more meaningful result. In contrast, educators should continuously strive to deploy the most appropriate teaching methods, bringing into the classroom the tools to respond to the fast-paced and ever-changing rhythm of society.

The Networked Urbanism studio adopted a framework of experiential education that promotes learning through direct action on the ground and reflection in a continuous feedback loop. With this approach, students actively engaged in posing questions, assuming responsibilities, being curious and creative, investigating, experimenting, and constructing meaning. They became intellectually, emotionally, and socially engaged. This involvement produced a perception that the learning process is authentic, necessary, and real.

Working in the real world meant that the results could not be predicted or controlled. For this reason, students had to take risks during the process, experiencing successes, frustrations, and uncertainties. In this context, the teacher became a supporter and advisor who guided students through a maze of difficulty and serendipity. In this process, network building, communication, and dialogue were essential.

As a starting point, the Networked Urbanism toolbox provided a set of guidelines that could be applied sequentially throughout the design process. It was meant to assist students in developing the skills necessary for this new reality and for the updated and expanded role that will be expected from them as designers.

#networkedurbanism design thinking methodology: a toolbox with 10 guidelines

1. EXPLORE: Choose a topic at the intersection between your personal interests and societal needs. Some students may already have an issue in mind that they feel passionately about, while others will have to research among the multiple layers of urban life until they find something that has both personal and societal relevance. By taking ownership of the project, they will be stimulated to generate innovative and ambitious ideas. Even ordinary life processes can provide an incredibly rich and fertile field for experimentation, while at the same time offering the potential to make a genuine difference in society. Designers can, and should, reach toward utopia even as they keep one foot firmly on the ground.

2. RESEARCH: Become an expert on the topic. The research process is open-ended. It is natural for the line of inquiry to evolve, taking on a life of its own, leading in directions that could not be foreseen at the beginning.

3. NETWORK: Create a network—from citizens to experts—and explore connections at both the official and grassroots level. Today's complex reality requires not just a multidisciplinary approach, but a transdisciplinary one, and the definition of new instruments, models, and protocols that cannot occur when professions work separately from one another. In the early stages of the project, students are encouraged to establish relationships with a variety of experts and stakeholders. They are asked to build networks of advisors and supporters from academia, the public and private sector, and potential community members. The progress of their projects depends on their ability to elicit the support and cooperation of these key players who often have different agendas. Suddenly, an internally-driven idea becomes a collaborative effort that contributes to its development.

4. SHARE: Confront and experience ideas outside your own desk—feedback is a treasure. It is extremely important to listen and engage in dialogue with people throughout the creative process. Incorporating feedback vastly enriches students' analysis of the issue, which by extension, ensures that their solutions are more relevant and viable.

5. BE OPEN: Start with a detailed plan but be prepared to disrupt it, responding to its natural development. There is a growing "culture of the process" that is making designers more aware of the implications of design, allowing them to acquire new inputs, incorporate feedback on the go, and make the required adjustments before the creative process is completely finished.

Students need to be very flexible in how they approach a problem and arrive at a solution. It is not a linear path from start to finish, but a dendritic one that follows an unpredictable course. It is extremely valuable for a designer's development to become comfortable with open-endedness and uncertainty. Reaching out and surfing reality introduces serendipity into the process, multiplying the possibilities for successful connections, making both the research and proposal more meaningful.

6. THINK BIG: Focus on a small-scale design that has the potential of the larger scale, and design a strategic overall vision. Big changes in the world happen incrementally. The best way to tackle a major societal problem is to begin with a manageable pilot project, while still envisioning a much larger scale strategy.

7. START SMALL: Any aspect can be the starting point; the concept will grow as your project develops. Students are encouraged to dive in as quickly as possible, without worrying too much about whether they are approaching the project in the "right" way. The important thing is not where to start, but simply to start. In keeping with the flexibility inherent in networked design, it is natural for things to change as the process unfolds, so there really is no single, correct way to begin.

8. ACT NOW!: Prototype and implement in real life at least a small but significant part of the design. It is important to put initiatives in motion. Action should come first, followed by reflection, in an ongoing feedback loop. The horizon is often blurry, but can only be reached by moving toward it. Prototyping an aspect of the design is a critical step so that eventually it can be scaled up.

9. COMMUNICATE: Take your initiative to a broader audience. By using today's digital technologies and the networks that they have created, students are able to extend the reach and impact of their proposals. In addition, they need to find the most powerful and appropriate way to spread the word about their initiative.

builders of smart networks, and thus, builders of smarter urban communities.

The Networked Urbanism teaching framework led to a myriad of outputs, with each project representing a singular response that reflected students' experiences, interests, and aspirations.

In this compilation, you will find different approaches and results, which respond to specific contexts and to each student's particular focus. Moreover, some of the projects

At this point, unexpected and exciting connections usually develop that propel the project much farther. Acquiring and applying skills in outreach and social networking are not typical aspects of a design school education, but are increasingly relevant for designers today.

10. MOVE BEYOND: How can you develop your project beyond the limits of the studio? The studio is a call to action: an invitation to join in the discussion beyond the doors of the classroom. As students see their proposals finding traction in the real world, they may be motivated to carry them forward even after the course is finished. The process they go through during the studio gives them the confidence to know that they can implement their ideas, and a willingness to push past their own preconceived limitations. Thus, the studio is an incubator for seed projects that have the capacity to grow beyond the academic term.

The goal of the Networked Urbanism studio was to encourage design students to contribute their knowledge and creativity to the spaces they live in, the communities they are a part of, and the issues they find important. The aim was also to teach them to be creative problem solvers,

that were developed within the studios are still "in progress" as they have grown beyond the boundaries of academia to become professional investigations and startups. Simultaneously and throughout the process, students naturally developed as entrepreneurs. The term *entreprene-ur-banism* arose in a conversation with a former student, and perfectly expresses the combination of these two concepts.

Due to their specificity and uniqueness, it is difficult to classify the projects by category, but there are some common themes among them such as: placemaking, digital tools, mapping, waste, mobility, resources, awareness, and education.

Teaching the Networked Urbanism studios has been an inspiring, fulfilling, and thrilling experience. We keep in touch with many of the participants and keep track of the development of their careers. We have great expectations for them. We have great expectations for achieving a better urban life. Hopefully, by reading this book, you will too.

Actual Air

Mike Styczynski

The ambition of this project responds to the context of apathy, detachment, and alienation individuals experience in response to challenges they face in urban environments. The project specifically focuses on air quality and the opportunities that sensor technology, low-cost do-it-yourself electronics, and social media enable individuals to explore, understand, and discuss within their communities. The current infrastructure of air-quality monitoring devices within Boston provides a misleading portrait of air quality, while the quality can be considered "good" on average, an understanding of the micro-environments we experience on a daily basis aren't adequately understood. This project provides the tools to explore these problem areas and serves as a template to imagine how individuals and communities can actively engage the public realm.

Current air monitoring infrastructure is removed from the personal environments in which people experience the city. The difficulty lies in the inability to target problem areas, which thus prevents the development of tools to deal with the issue at the level of lived experience. In certain instances, air pollution related to automobile and diesel exhaust dissipates exponentially, complicating the ability to understand how this pollution affects an entire neighborhood. The development of a broad-based network of individually-controlled sensors provides a measure of personal experience as well as a measure of specific place.

Research methods and project approaches are developed in two forms. The first is con-cerned with creating the processes and spaces necessary to enable participation and engagement. While citizen science efforts have a mixed history, this work is less about collecting legitimate data than it is about empowering individuals with the tools necessary to understand the different ways that data can be collected and transmitted. Empowerment cannot be considered authentic unless the individual has the capacity to decide how and if information is communicated, and to whom. The second form of this work is about creating the tools necessary to enable the measurement of air quality. These tools are built upon a conceptualized set of open-source and readily available parts, which can be expanded upon to produce a variety of configu-

"Empowering individuals with the tools necessary to not only collect data, but also understand the different ways that data can be collected and transmitted."

rations. This DIY kit is intended to be flexible in order to allow for personal reconfiguration and functionality in a variety of contexts.

The project functions in two ways. The first is through the development of a conceptual framework that focuses on enabling individual agency through the control and design of devices that can measure multiple parameters and produce multiple types of outputs. It is essential within the project that the outputting of information is controlled by the individual who is interested in bringing the resources and tools necessary to measure air quality within their environment and experience of urban space. This control of information is the first step in creating quality data. In this context, quality means something entirely different than in a research context. Here, the quality of information needs to meet certain empirical criteria, but more importantly has to be meaningful to the user. That is to say, the data should be directly connected to how people experience urban space, and should reflect the variety of experiences people have within the city. Data collected at the top of a building may be precise, but in the larger scope this does little to enhance the understanding of air quality as it is experienced by individuals.

The conceptual kit of parts can in effect produce a wide range of possible tools to measure air quality. The focus of the project takes advantage of these as an existing cultural artifact with a broad range of relationships and subcultures that are clustered around them. One of the fundamental purposes of the bicycle prototype is to produce an evocative image and display, which is designed to encourage and provoke the imagination about the potential of the project. The incorporation of the bicycle as an element of the project capitalizes on an existing cultural platform that already forms the basis of shared social identity among individuals and certain subcultures. These subcultures range from hipsters, to "SCUL," to road bicycling enthusiasts. Every person has a vision for how

they would incorporate the basic structure of the project into their experience of cycling and urban space. In a sense the bike becomes the armature for the deployment of the device in strategic locations. The bike is part of an imagined set of tools that are "rented" for the price of passing learned knowledge and information on to the next person who is interested in using the bike. The underlying goal is to promote exchange among users of the device, and to encourage the development of a robust and extensive network of interested individuals. The prototypes thus become generators that can catalyze the imagination of a wider audience. This results from the flexibility of the project which allows it to be adapted to the interests of different individuals and subcultures within the broader community of bicycle enthusiasts. In this way the practice of data capture is revolutionized by collective, yet individualized research.

Top: Testing model with DIY electronics

Bottom: Measuring CO_2, H_2, and uncombusted hydrocarbons from unfiltered Lucky Strikes

Testing the device on a bike

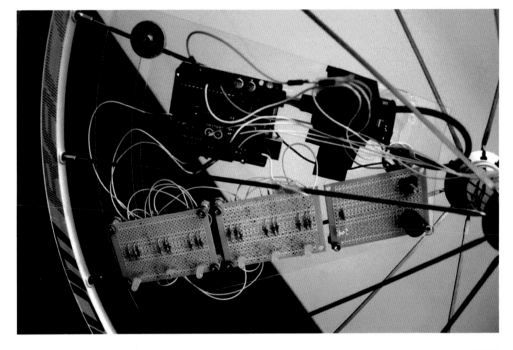

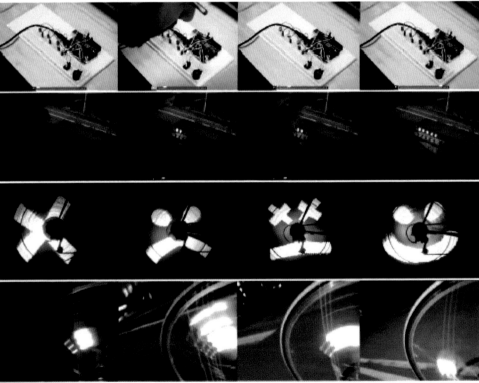

Top: Close-up of the
bike-mounted device

Bottom: Conceptual kit that can
measure multiple parameters and
produce multiple types of outputs

Right: Air quality data collection,
color index

BASE

CLEAR

OK

PROBLEMATIC

iBike Boston

Andrew P. Leonard

iBike questions both the practice of data collection as well as the dissemination of information. By mounting specific sensors to a bicycle, data was collected in an effort to draw the experience of cyclists in Boston. Using an accelerometer to measure micro-topography and a GPS to geolocate the information and to provide speed data, iBike improves on existing cycling maps by redrawing the city based on the experience of cycling. The resulting maps provide cyclists with a layer of information that is currently absent in existing cycle maps, and that relates directly to human experience.

iBike Boston began with a simple proposition: go out and explore Boston, to discover the city. This seemed a funny proposition as Boston is my home, where I have lived and worked for eight years, having grown up in a smaller city 15 minute to the south. Accepting the challenge of discovering my city I decided to take my bike and ride around the residential part of South Boston. I have spent quite a bit of time in Southie, but always along the water or along Broadway, the main street running through the middle. What I found was that it was nearly impossible to get from my apartment in the South End to South Boston, a distance of only about two miles. Though Boston has been making great strides to become a more cyclable city, major gaps in the infrastructure and linkages still exist. The two mile ride to Southie takes you across a four lane intersection, then onto a ramp over the highway, and finally around a major rotary. The way back takes you under the highway where no cross lanes exist.

This adventure got me thinking about how different the rhetoric about Boston being a more cyclable city is from the actual experience of riding. I began looking at maps, both cycle-specific as well as common digital maps. The cycle maps that I found provided little information on what the surficial conditions actually were. Cycle lanes, if represented at all,

"The resulting maps provide the cyclist with a layer of information that relates directly to human experience."

were simply demarcated by color coded lines transposed on top of street centerlines, providing no information about their width or quality. The base maps that the diagrammatic overlays were applied to were similarly simplified, seemingly dependent on satellite imagery to provide any "real" surficial information. The ubiquitous Google map that everyone is familiar with stands as a contradiction to the vast amount of data that is available. The flattened surface of the "map view" juxtaposed with the satellite imagery layer are presented as a complete picture of the world, encompassing all of the resolution necessary. With this combination of the ultra-simplified map and satellite imagery, a certain thickness of information that had been drawn into maps for centuries has been wiped away. Furthermore, the ubiquity of data collection devices (smartphones with GPS, etc.) brings to question why modern cartography has largely been simplified (perhaps because of the ubiquity of data collection and dissemination).

From this research I decided to explore how a thicker, more informative cycle map could be drawn—to remap the city based on the experience of cycling. To do this I built a sensor to mount on my bike in order to map data related to the experience of the ride. I focused on two parameters: micro-topography and speed. For micro-topography, I used an accelerometer that allowed me to take the z-value from the inertia sensor and was thus able to map the feeling of the road while riding. A GPS was used to geolocate the information and to provide speed data. The width of roads is drawn based on the speed of travel (faster roads feel wider) and the micro-topography is expressed by varied mark densities when viewed at the neighborhood scale and as a color gradation at the larger scale. The resulting maps provide the cyclist with a layer of information absent in existing cycle maps that relates directly to the human experience. The limited parameters of micro-topography and speed provide information pertinent to cyclists, as they are two major factors in the comfort of a

ride. Additionally, the use of the accelerometer and GPS allows for future scalability as most, if not all, smartphones have these two sensors built in. With the intention of turning this into a crowd-sourcing app, iBike can redraw the city based on the experience of cycling temporally, showing conditions as they change. The maps have the ability to evolve as roads change, as construction begins or ends, or even diurnally, so that cyclists can have a better understanding of what the riding conditions are likely to be at any given time.

This project was selected for further development by the Harvard Innovation Lab, and was a finalist for the 2013 President's Challenge.

3 AXIS ACCELEROMETER
z-axis data used to map micro-topography

GPS UNIT
geolocates data and provides speed of travel

SD LOGGER
logs data from trip

ARDUINO
microprocessor, controls the sensor

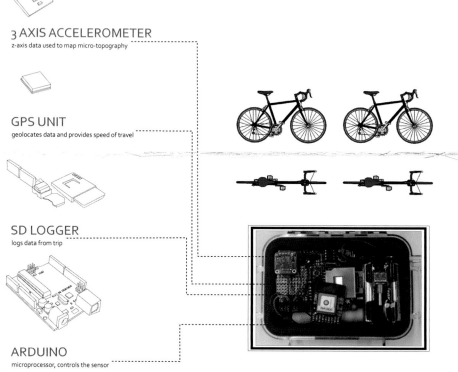

Explanation

slow road   fast road

smooth road   rough road

distance from start location

Top: iBike prototype

Bottom: Map showing the georeferenced collected data

Right: iBike adapted to the existing local Hubway SmartBike system in the Boston metro area

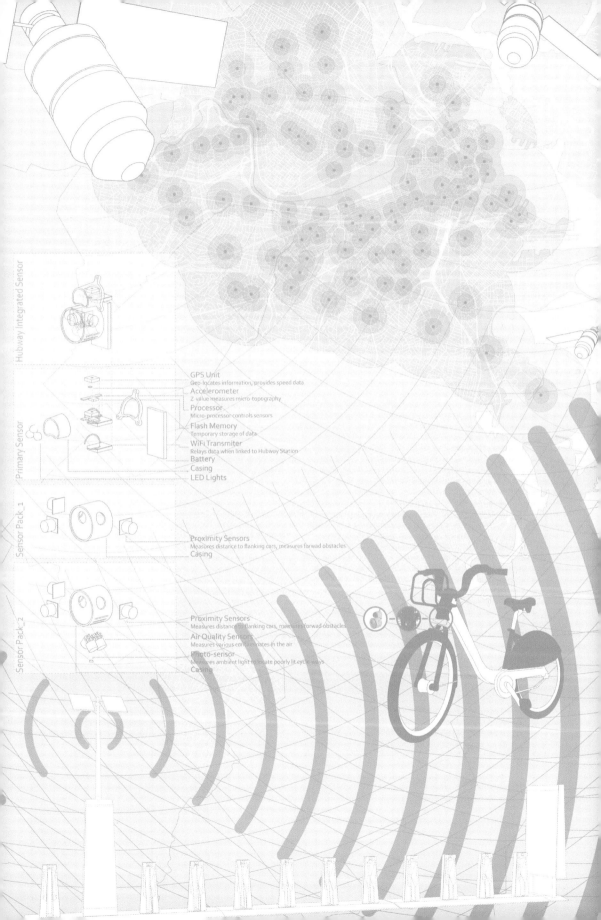

Hubway Integrated Sensor

Primary Sensor

GPS Unit
Geo-locates information, provides speed data
Accelerometer
Z-value measures micro-topography
Processor
Micro-processor controls sensors
Flash Memory
Temporary storage of data
WiFi Transmiter
Relays data when linked to Hubway Station
Battery
Casing
LED Lights

Sensor Pack_1

Proximity Sensors
Measures distance to flanking cars, measures forwad obstacles
Casing

Sensor Pack_2

Proximity Sensors
Measures distance to flanking cars, measures forwad obstacles
Air Quality Sensors
Measures various contaminates in the air
Photo-sensor
Measures ambient light to locate poorly lit cycle ways
Casing

tagmesave.me

Krystelle Denis
Ziyi Zhang

Inventorying is essential for reducing waste at the Harvard Recycling and Surplus Center, where reuse is distributed back to the community. However, the process is very labor intensive and time consuming. In collaboration with the facility, the project calls for a cooperative networked inventorying of surplus to minimize individual workload and maximize item order and distribution, thus minimizing waste.

The project aims to reduce the trashing of Harvard surplus by increasing item reuse. Waste and surplus travel to the Harvard Recycling and Surplus Center, which distributes reuse to the Harvard community and nonprofit organizations. However, in order to store new surplus, room must be made by trashing older surplus that cannot be recycled or scrapped. The wasted surplus ends up in landfills, harming our ecosystem.

Inventorying is essential for reducing Harvard waste. Creating physical order along with an itemized list, report, or record of things helps the facility keep track of what's in stock and allows collectors (artists, furniture collectors, computer tinkerers, nonprofit organizations, and scrap metal collectors) to understand what is available to them. However, inventorying is currently very labor intensive and time consuming for the Harvard Recycling and Surplus Center.

The staff voiced that they would like help in simplifying their searching and inventorying procedures as well as reaching out to a larger community through digitizing these processes. Although once in a while they use Craigslist, this method is too time-consuming and inefficient for large quantities.

The project implementation is adapted to work with the facility's new warehouse and surplus management procedures. Surplus will be ordered by day and time, and divided by week, in order to track how long the items have been

"By distributing the workload of inventorying to a larger community of online users, the documented surplus can become a sophisticated dynamic catalog that adapts to user interests."

sitting in the facility, and to know how to prioritize them.

Inventorying is split into two main processes: offline inventorying and online inventorying. After the items are stored, offline inventorying is performed by the Harvard Recycling and Surplus Center with a phone application (TMSM). As surplus streams into the facility, they can be quickly photographed and uploaded to the online database, where they are publicly displayed and assigned a unique ID (ex: 2013-12-12-13-5712, year-month-day-hour-minute-second), a reference to the item's location in the facility. Once they are uploaded, the online inventorying is performed by the community through the website tagmesave.me. The website users perform collaborative inventorying of surplus by tagging—a rapid process of attaching words that describe the item, such as its color, shape, material, texture, brand, or the like.

Collaborative inventorying is done using a technique called human-based computing, which generally outsources certain steps of the computing process to humans; this approach uses differences in abilities between humans and computers to achieve symbiotic human-computer interaction. In this case, recognizing things is quite hard for computer software but easy for a person, therefore the computer manages the database but tagging is outsourced to a community of users, so each individual effort is minimal.

By distributing the workload of inventorying to a larger community of online users, the documented surplus can become a sophisticated dynamic catalog that adapts to user interests. This allows users to find the items they need through a database keyword search engine, discover related items with similar tags, and build relationships between items. Once a user finds the item, they can "save it" or "claim it" online, allowing them to locate it within the facility using the unique ID provided.

This digital intervention will demonstrate the positive impact of reusing surplus and strengthen symbiosis between the Harvard community and the Harvard Recycling and Surplus Center. The project will enable the Harvard departments to keep track of the surplus they produce, and become aware of which items have been reused or sent to a landfill. The collected data generated through the website will allow for the studying of interactions among website users, and between users and surplus, and therefore for the discovery of new patterns. The Harvard community could ultimately use these revealed surplus and waste patterns for future reference and adjustments, and for the creation of a waste memory.

During the studio this team obtained a grant from the Harvard Office for Sustainability to develop the project.

Top: Workers sorting goods at
the Harvard Recycling and Surplus
Center warehouse

Bottom: Harvard Recycling and
Surplus Center warehouse

Right: Cooperative networked
inventorying diagram

Cooperative Networked Inventorying

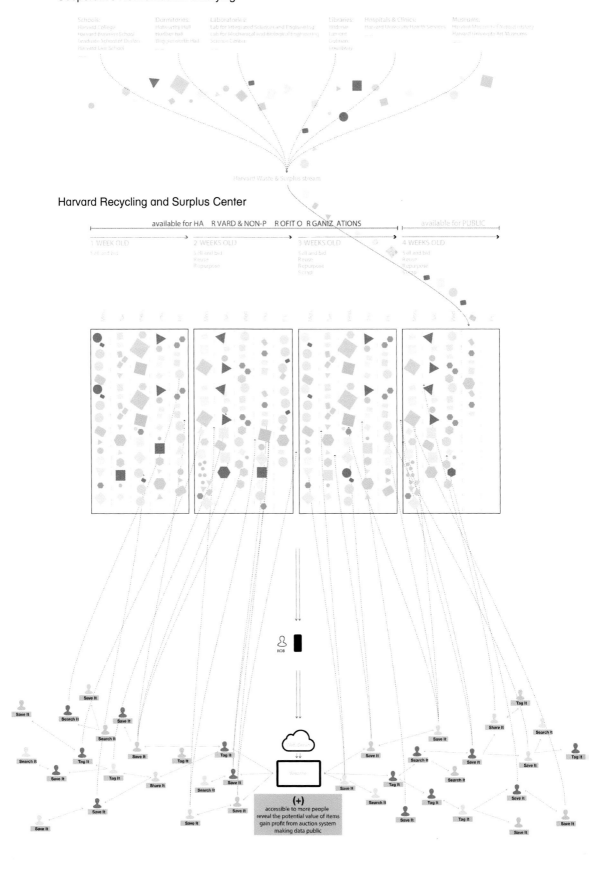

Schools:
Harvard College
Harvard Business School
Graduate School of Design
Harvard Law School

Dormitories:
Hollworthy Hall
Hurlbut Hall
Wigglesworth Hall

Laboratories:
Lab for Integrated Sciences and Engineering
Lab for Mechanical and Biological Engineering
Science Center

Libraries:
Widener
Lamont
Gutman
Loeb Music

Hospitals & Clinics:
Harvard University Health Services

Museums:
Harvard Museum of Natural History
Harvard University Art Museums

Harvard Waste & Surplus stream

Harvard Recycling and Surplus Center

available for HARVARD & NON-PROFIT ORGANIZATIONS   available for PUBLIC

1 WEEK OLD	2 WEEKS OLD	3 WEEKS OLD	4 WEEKS OLD
Sell and bid	Sell and bid
Reuse
Repurpose	Sell and bid
Reuse
Repurpose
Scrap	Sell and bid
Reuse
Repurpose

(+)
accessible to more people
reveal the potential value of items
gain profit from auction system
making data public

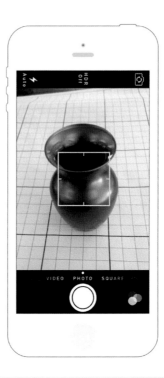

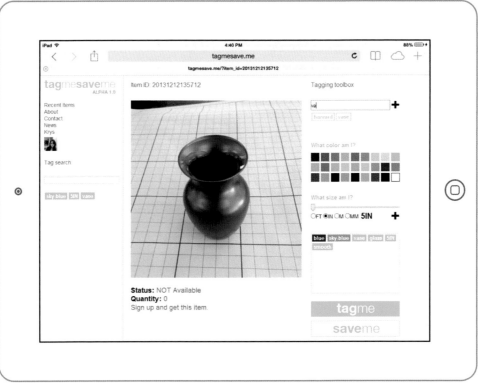

Top: First step, offline inventorying: objects are photographed and uploaded to the website's online database

Bottom: Second step, online inventorying: the objects are tagged by the community on the website through collaborative tagging

Right: tagmesave.me webpage

tagmesaveme

Krystelle Denis + Ziyi Zhang

tagmesaveme
ALPHA 1.0

Recent items
About
Contact
News
Sign In

Tag search:

chair speakers keyboard
white magenta blue
Breuer charcoal-grey
yellow silver-gray black
office leather rolling
microwave cooking
appliance womens
clothing sweater dress
laptop-bag aqua 3FT 2FT
wood brown red
mint-green light-pink scarf
115IN glossy book
melon-pink light-yellow
women psychology
peter-gray beige
long-sleeved-shirt harvard
gold orange vintage Dell
025FT Charger Lenovo
6IN 5FT metal mesh
shelf upholstered wheels
plastic Santa hat
Christmas plush rounded
filing cabinet drawers
Cesca dance theatre
1990s lime-green 0IN
IMac usb desk oak
golden-oak 4-drawer
alien-worlds super-earth
sasselov scale detecto
grey lance-armstrong
bestseller wilcockson
bloom happy-trails
bloom-county
berke-breathed paperback
pullover purple fluffy
computer-speakers
paperroll desk-chair
coffee-table modern
well-worn Horror Volume-II
Crime-and-Horror board
computerbag 36MM 225IN
lumber 4IN forest-green
chinese-book girlfriends
jeans agenda 10IN
rolling-cart stained
with-arms glove comfort
975FT loud Shirt
sky-blue music stool
violet shiny 5IN vase
kitchen wooden table
slim glass smooth copier
dining oval cozy
cardboard 25FT
shorter-plays binder
24-volts ii766 Tube 8IN
IPHONE light-blue 1075IN
magazine-or-book 575FT
backpack leaf-green 0M
binders coat-rack hat-tree
file-cabinet winter jacket
onesie baby bear boots
ski law text-book writing
modernism 15MM speaker
2225MM CD 14MM
furniture lights electronics
Electronic Radio Wool
Striped .325FT 1FT Child
Coat Viking beckett
particleboard painted

New items

Curbed City

Christopher M. Johnson
Jean You

50

Every year on September 1st, the city of Cambridge experiences mass migration—creating over 5 percent of the city's waste in one day. Unlike regular trash, the majority of this waste is furniture that is in good condition and typically just a few years old. Within the same time frame that people are moving out, new residents, typically first-year college students, are purchasing the same items, only to be trashed a few years later. Curbed City is a way to intervene in this cycle by providing an open-source Web-based platform that utilizes current behavioral patterns while allowing those who need items to acquire them easily within their current neighborhood.

Cambridge is home to numerous world-class universities including Harvard and MIT, and over 105,000 residents that can be broken apart into three distinct groups: professionals, a strong working class, and the largest segment with over 40 percent, students. The governing bodies including the city and the universities are plagued with misaligned interests exposed through their resource allocation and differentiation of waste streams. Through quantitative and qualitative research including numerous interviews with a variety of stakeholders—people in the municipal office, MIT, and Harvard—and a survey that was completed by over 180 students and residents across the city, our research showed that the city has been left "holding the bag" at the end of the day. From each stakeholder's perspective, waste

> **"Curbed City began as a platform that would curb the waste that is created around September 1st, which accounts for 5 percent of the city's entire annual waste."**

was merely a byproduct of inconvenience. This perception spans each socioeconomic group that was contacted, and each institution, no matter how large or small—it is a matter of convenience.

This discovery, novel at best, led us to look for a moment to intervene within the system— one that is universal and would capitalize on current behaviors that could morph based upon the time of year, or the needs of the users.

Initially, Curbed City began as a platform that would curb the waste created around September 1st. Most importantly, unlike standard household waste, what is disposed around this date has a very high value. Also, there is a high correlation between this furniture waste and attempted alternate disposal methods including gifting, Craigslist, and multiple phone calls to different donation centers. And, due to the heavy proportionality of students who stay in the city on average just over three years, their furniture and household items are typically in good condition upon disposal, and incoming classes frequently purchase the same items.

Moving forward from this notion, in order to further develop the platform, additional research was done to study current and proposed city and institutional policies as well as the best practices used across the country for not only recycling, but also acquiring used items. The systems and channels were quite similar, and subsequently the City of Cambridge's systems work efficiently when treating all items as waste, yet they failed to address the greater needs of the community. The key to a successful program is to capitalize on current behavioral patterns the city is all too familiar with, and make a spectacle of it. It must create a platform that embraces the street, the needs, and consumption and waste habits of the residents as a public performance that does not penalize people for handing off their goods to the next user but chooses the most convenient, safe, and accessible local approach. The current Curbed City is a platform that has the ability to revolutionize not only how we "freecycle" furniture, but how we view the city and its use

of goods and commodity patterns along with the notions of furniture and the realms of personal and business relationships, art, and even pop-up events. In future generations of the platform, we see the system expanding to include a whole host of additional features that will maintain the streamlined aesthetic and functionality that has been designed but will include scheduling abilities, donation specifications, and alerts when desired items become available. This is just the beginning of how Curbed City can embrace the urban context and allow its participants to map a city by its' commodities, trades, and interactions.

This project is currently being developed with the City of Cambridge Department of Public Works.

Top: Proposed "curbed" flow

Bottom: Trashed furniture on the
streets of Cambridge, September 1

Step 1   Step 2   Step 3

Top: App screenshot showing
available furniture   Bottom: The app in use

Carbon Counting

James W. Perakis

Carbon counters—in both physical and digital form—are meant to stimulate discussion about carbon emissions and climate change at the GSD. The impact that our buildings have on the environment is an issue that is often glossed over at the school as it is in most public discussions. If we want to address our concerns for the environment, issues of climate change need to be brought into our collective consciousness, and that starts with raising awareness about our own carbon footprint.

This semester began with an assumption that educating the public about the way our built environment works, specifically the way it uses energy and contributes to the problem of global warming, has the potential to correct some of our more problematic behaviors. One component of education is finding ways to visualize the invisible yet ubiquitous energy infrastructure and how that infrastructure operates. The other is to visualize the real-time impact our buildings have on the environment, and in so doing affect the decisions we make regarding how we interact with the built world.

While there are undoubtedly many ways to communicate this information, the studio was an opportunity to experiment with an unfamiliar medium: animation. The first experiment involved an animation describing the movement of energy from the point of resource extraction to the point of consumption (the city of Boston). Since Boston, like many northeastern cities, creates most of its useable energy from burning natural gas, the animation begins in the Mississippi Delta where most of the nation's natural gas is processed before it travels via one of several large pipelines to the electric generation facility. The fact that Boston relies heavily on natural gas for its electric generation is an important point, because it enables one to calculate the amount of carbon created per kilowatt-hour of electricity generated.

This first animation was an introduction to new tools and new techniques of representation. While it was an informative exercise, it failed to

"Educating the public about the way our built environment uses energy has the potential to correct some of our more problematic behaviors."

communicate the urgency of reducing our collective energy footprint. The description of resource movement from source to sink was ultimately too abstract and removed from the everyday behaviors of ordinary citizens. Using the lessons learned from this first iteration, the second animation used data collected from actual buildings to concretize what was formerly too abstract.

Even with the complexities involved in the processes of energy generation and transmission (deregulated markets, interconnected power grids, etc.), collecting and animating information about how specific buildings or groups of individuals use energy is decidedly more difficult. In order to streamline the research, Gund Hall served as a test kitchen because of its pseudo-open data portal to energy monitoring systems. Real-time data on everything from lighting loads to steam use is continuously collected, packaged, and then e-mailed as a text file once a day. Using this information, the numbers in the animation are presented in traditional terms, such as kilowatt-hours for lighting and therms for heating, as well as comparative figures such as number of houses powered per year. For example, the amount of energy used to light Gund Hall is equal to the amount of energy it would take to power 208 medium-sized houses. The numbers and figures are also presented in relation to other buildings on the Harvard campus as a way to accentuate the point that Gund uses more energy per square foot than almost any other building in the area except the Science Center (and most of this energy goes toward unnecessarily lighting the building during all hours of the day).

This animation played in the GSD café, the Chauhaus, alongside a device that reads the (almost) real-time carbon emissions of Gund Hall. Although the output from this carbon counter is a simple number, the device was designed as an object of intrigue that people could walk up to and investigate—a dynamic and slightly more interactive type of informative poster.

These types of displays are particularly important for the design school, since we as designers are rarely confronted with the reality of how our creations impact the environment. Buildings account for almost half of all carbon emissions in the United States, and designers have a responsibility to create an efficient and responsible built environment. If an awareness of energy use becomes part of our consciousness as designers, and if we are constantly reminded of the ways in which our creations use energy, we are more likely to design and create a better built environment for the future.

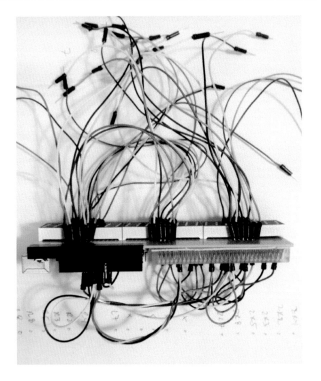

Top: Carbon Counting device showing the amount of carbon dioxide emitted since January 1, 2012 at the GSD

Bottom: The device being assembled

Right: Graphics from the animation showing the energy consumption and carbon dioxide emissions of various buildings on the Harvard campus

395,304
LBS CO₂
YEAR

 + 🖥️

$37,349
YEAR

+

+

+

GEORGE GUND HALL

$ 545,722

UTILITY COSTS (2010)

CHILLED WATER		20 %
ELECTRICTY		50 %
NATURAL GAS		0 %
STEAM		30 %

Trashy Behavior

Josh Westerhold

Our lives are filled with choices. From the rare and complicated to the mundane, we venture through life moving from one decision to the next. Often we take time to consider our options, choosing the path that provides maximum utility; however, many of our decisions are made with little thought to cost or consequence. When taken alone these decisions can be overlooked, but if these decisions reveal a pattern across a community they magnify into material harm. Trashy Behavior is a project determined to shift trash choices toward more sustainable solutions and improve our world, one community at a time.

When I began this project, I was interested in investigating individual decisions that create a network of consequences in our cities. By bringing together urban planning and design with the field of behavioral science I believed I could identify a specific moment of individual choice that is replicated often enough that any shift in behavior could have a material impact. With the guidance of two behavioral scientists, Todd Rogers and Erin Frey, I began considering moments such as commuting choice, shopping behavior, and digital mapping; however, daily interaction with a public display of bad design took me on an unexpected path.

In Chauhaus, our café at the GSD, I noticed how difficult it was to decide where to throw my trash. The large, public trash station seemed designed with proper sorting in mind but had little understanding of behavior. The signage was a confusing mess of small images including both what does and does not go in each bin. Conversations with my peers confirmed that I wasn't alone in my confusion, so I decided to observe the pattern scientifically. After indiscreetly filming the trash station during several lunch rushes, I was not surprised to see person after person showing signs of confusion. A 2010 waste audit at the GSD confirmed my suspicion that when

"Trash is a choice."

people are confused, they default to the easiest option, the trash bin. Here was my opportunity to test my theory that relatively small interventions could scale across a community for noticeable change.

Knowing little about waste I sought out the expertise of Robert Gogan, Director of Recycling and Waste Services at Harvard, as well as Trevor O'Brien, Assistant Facilities Manager at the GSD and a member of the Harvard Green Team. Realizing that I could not intervene without a personal understanding of my own habits, I created a commitment device known as Trashless Tuesdays. Similar to Meatless Mondays, my goal was to stop producing trash at least one day a week, a 15 percent reduction in my own waste footprint. I then created a plan for intervention and scheduled a new waste audit to test the results. The most obvious intervention was to redesign the trash station at Chauhaus. I did this by simplifying the display to show only what went in the recycle and compost bins and attaching the negative association of the giant word "landfill" to the trash bin. However, I also knew that a significant amount of trash was improperly disposed of in the rest of the building, away from the Chauhaus trash station. To shift this behavior I decided on a public awareness campaign of stickers placed in conspicuous locations around the GSD. Using behavioral techniques such as anchoring, social norms, and self-perception theory these stickers were intended to prompt conversation and awareness. Each of the stickers included the message "Trash is a choice" along with the hashtag #trashlesstuesdays, in the hope that this might translate into a digital conversation as well.

The week of rollout I recorded the lunch rush at the Chauhaus station and saw a more efficient use of the station. I also conducted a waste audit in the Pit at the GSD. This very public display of our trash was met with conversation and even outright consternation. Despite this being the trash produced by our community in the GSD, this was now a "biohazard." The audit served its purpose as public shaming and performance art, as crowds stood around watching their peers dressed like lab technicians dig through and resort their trash. The interventions were successful in producing a material behavior change, as we saw a 40 percent increase in composting accuracy and a 140 percent increase in recycling accuracy!

It is certainly a success to have this kind of behavior change in a controlled environment, but how can we impact "trashy behavior" more universally? One option I have begun to consider looks at the 100 million tons of building and construction materials we throw in landfills every year. Taking a cue from the shadow boxes at Chauhaus, what if we knew what was in every building and whether it was recyclable or reusable before demolition? How could this impact the behavior of the development and building trades? Could we create a more efficient market for these products and shift global behavior away from disposable materials to reuse? I don't know the answers yet, but my experience this semester gives me reason to hope that with simple interventions our behavior doesn't have to be so trashy.

Top: Campaign stickers

Bottom: Waste audit in the
Pit at the GSD

Top: Campaign stickers

Bottom: The new trash station
at the Chauhaus

Aquaplot

Jennifer Corlett
Kelly Murphy

Aquaplot uses discarded oyster shells from local restaurants to sustain oyster reefs and reestablish a healthy harbor ecosystem via a citywide oyster gardening program that closes the oyster waste stream, restores native oyster reefs, improves local water quality, and reconnects the people of Boston with their waterfront.

To many people, Boston is synonymous with shellfish, especially oysters. Oysters have always been a cornerstone of the New England diet, and were once a mainstay in the Boston harbor. Oyster reefs were a crucial element of the underwater landscape that filtered our estuaries and maintained our harbor as a rich natural resource area. They not only clean water, but also act as shoreline buffers that dissipate wave energy. What's more, they support critical fisheries by providing habitat for numerous fish and crustacean species. Oyster reefs, however, are now the most severely impacted marine habitat on earth: over 85 percent have been lost globally.

Today, we hear a lot about oysters, whether it's their ability to bolster coastlines in the face of climate change, their water filtration capabilities

(the average adult oyster can filter 50 gallons of water per day), their potential for remediating eutrophic waters, or the food culture surrounding their consumption. There is, however, an important gap in this discourse: what about the waste associated with their consumption? What happens to oyster shells once they've been discarded?

Most people don't recognize the magnitude of waste associated with discarded oyster shells once they're consumed. In Massachusetts alone, 4.1 million pounds of oysters were harvested last year. Over 40 restaurants in Boston serve oysters, lending a distinctive identity to our city. Each restaurant generates around 20 pounds of oyster shells per day. Together, this totals over 300,000 pounds of oyster shells per year in Boston alone. Of these 40-plus Boston restaurants, only four

> **"Oyster gardening can simultaneously restore native oyster reefs, improve local water quality, and reconnect the people of Boston with their waterfront."**

recycle their shells, meaning that 90 percent of shells are currently landfilled. Why? Because Boston doesn't yet have a place for its shells.

How do you use discarded shells to sustain oyster reefs and reestablish a healthy harbor ecosystem? By establishing a citywide oyster gardening program that can close the gap in the oyster waste stream by creating demand for discarded shells. Oyster gardening can simultaneously restore native oyster reefs, improve local water quality, and reconnect the people of Boston with their waterfront. There are a number of successful precedents for oyster gardening programs around the region. There is no reason why Boston shouldn't be at the forefront of oyster gardening given its rich heritage.

Boston is known for its shellfish; however, it is not performing well on the shell recycling front. Within this broken cycle lies an opportunity for Boston to address two key problems: wasted shells and oyster reef decline. While there are numerous productive uses for discarded oyster shells, the best use by far is as reef substrate to grow juvenile oysters. The link between the two problems presents an exciting opportunity to propose a better system.

The waters of the Boston Harbor are currently closed to shell fishing due to the risk of oysters being harvested illegally in polluted waters. However, nursery areas for shellfish seeding projects are permitted if they are transplanted to approved waters. Over the last three years, the Massachusetts Oyster Project has proven that oysters can survive in Boston Harbor. In just a few years, oyster gardeners could use discarded restaurant shells to grow thousands of oysters in the Boston Harbor and restock endangered reefs in the region.

The benefits of oyster gardening are manifold, and span environmental, economic, and social realms. Oyster gardening connects the waste source to the solution, revives Boston's local heritage, reconnects people with their waterfront, and brings life back to Boston Harbor.

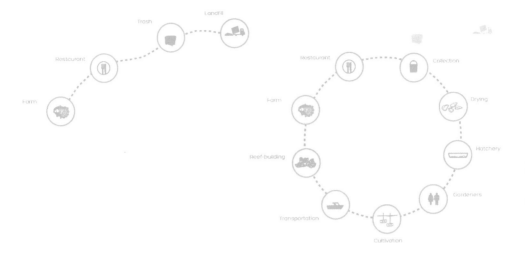

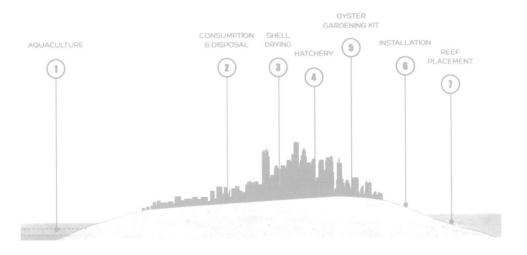

Top: Current oyster cycle and proposed closed cycle

Middle: Oyster gardening kit

Bottom: The cycle through the city

Jennifer Corlett + Kelly Murphy

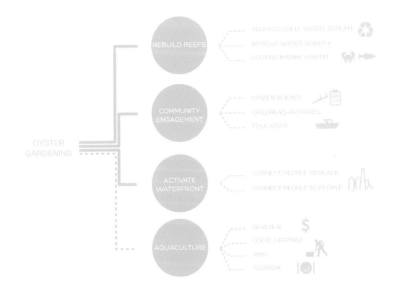

Top: Diagram showing agents
involved in oyster gardening

Bottom: Image of what
Boston could look like

Know Your Water

Karyssa K. Halstead

Through their water usage, Bostonians are one part of an extensive, connected system. The delivery of water to and from your home comprises more resources than water alone and results in large-scale infrastructural interventions that shape our landscape and impact ecosystems on both sides of the chain. By exploring methods of communicating these concepts, I hope to provide a tool that educates users as to what resources go into the treatment and transport of water, how they're using water in their homes, and why it's important to conserve it.

Know Your Water emerged out of an interest in the hidden infrastructure of the city. Cities have complicated networks of resources that lie beneath them and only through the occasional clue, such as a manhole cover, are we even aware of their existence. Water, electricity, and gas all appear at the click of a switch as if by magic; their supporting infrastructure is only questioned when there are problems. I was particularly interested in the water network of Boston due to the sheer size of its supporting infrastructure. Reservoirs and aqueducts are incredibly large interventions and Boston has one of the largest manmade reservoirs in the world. How have these massive landscape interventions been so successfully removed from our consciousness?

The first half of the semester was devoted to demystifying the water network, understanding all of the pieces of the potable water system from collection to use with the ultimate goal of targeting issues within the system that need to be communicated to the public. Since people tend to be very proactive about pushing for improve-

> **"If an awareness of where our water goes can be achieved, then perhaps we can start to make smarter choices about our usage and what we put down the drain."**

ments in visible infrastructure such as streets, I hoped that I could help encourage them to take an equal interest in their water infrastructure and push for improvements in the aging underground network.

Through research and interviews I realized that most of the issues in the Boston area lie not within the potable water networks, but post-use in the sewers. For example, combined sewer/storm water overflow pipes are driving the design of our sewer systems and wastewater treatment plants, causing major inefficiencies in the system especially during large storm events. Additionally, due to old pipes, clean water is infiltrating into the sewers, which, combined with a largely impervious surface, are lowering the ground water level causing wood pilings in buildings. However, the most essential piece of information I found was that the knowledge gap between the user and the water system is significant. Partially due to the abundance of rain in the region, clean water is majorly undervalued and many users don't understand why they should conserve it or even pay for it.

Currently, the average person pays only 1 to 2 cents per gallon for tap water in the Boston metropolitan area. Considering that as our population grows water is only going to get scarcer and prices cannot remain so deeply subsidized indefinitely, the goal of the project shifted to address the education of the average user toward the larger infrastructural, resource, and ecological requirements of water usage.

The infrastructural requirements to provide water to the entire Boston metropolitan area are obviously quite extensive. There are three water sources feeding the system: the Quabbin Reservoir, the Wachusett Reservoir, and the Ware River. Much of the land that drains into these sources, especially the Quabbin and Wachusett, is protected and came at the cost of displacement of multiple towns. Additionally, the water travels at least 80 miles from collection to ocean release in pipes that range from 4 inches to 23 feet in diameter.

There are also many other resources required in this process. A huge amount of energy is necessary to pump and treat wastewater and despite many efforts to use renewable resources as often as possible by the Massachusetts Water Resources Authority, 84 percent of the energy they use is still coming from power plants. There are also several chemicals that go into the water treatment process, disinfecting and altering the water composition.

Perhaps most important is the understanding that our water usage is part of a larger connected system. Our use affects ecosystems on both sides of the chain, and if an awareness of where our water goes can be achieved, then perhaps we can start to make smarter choices about our usage and what we put down the drain.

Know Your Water is not just about the water system alone, but is also an exercise in effectively conveying information. Much of my research is available through various water authorities' websites but is not presented in an easily accessible format. The process of water usage is complicated and systemic; the typical diagram is not effective at communicating these types of overlapping processes. Through a reiterative method, I used animation as a tool for experimentation in communication. The resulting short animation hopefully not only explains the process to users, but by presenting the information in a neutral way, asks people to have an opinion about it.

Above: Street art showing
Boston water basins

Right: Screenshots from the animation
showing main water resources, usage,
and energy costs for water treatment

38% WACHUSETT

13% WARE RIVER

53% QUABBIN

15.2% UNACCOUNTED FOR
(UN-METERED) WATER

0.2% OTHER

0.1% AGRICULTURAL

8.7% MUNICIPAL

2.5% INDUSTRIAL

15.5% COMMERCIAL

57.8% RESIDENTIAL

the majority of this water is used in homes

44.6miles

+ 2,568,000 kwh/ye

DEER ISLAND WATER TREATMENT PLANT

+ 28,000,000   methane recapture
+ 2,400,000   wind power
+ 284,000   solar power
+ 6,000,000   hydro power
- 128,716,000   total electrical demand

70.4miles

TOTAL ENERGY USE   -67,864,000 kwh/ye

My Little Public

Hung Kai Liao

My Little Public is a program that encourages a discussion that could form a new concept of future urban spaces. By educating children while they are young, we can foster their desire to cultivate an engaging and livable environment. It is a prospect of promoting a culture where people have more awareness and interaction with their environment.

In recent years, our lives have drastically been altered by the development of the information age. Thirty years ago, people could not have imagined a world of computer networks, smart-phones, and a staggering number of wireless technologies. For instance, in the 1990s, when making a date with a friend, you might say: "Let's meet right at the east entrance of Memo-rial Park at 7:00 sharp." But in 2010, you would say: "Let's meet in the Quincy area at around seven-ish, just call me or text me when you are in the area." In fact, the development of the information age has not only changed the way we live but how we perceive and interact with physical spaces. Instead of planning precisely, now you can freely meander in that area and just make sure your mobile phone is on and con-nected. In this new age, how will our physical environment add up to the new perception of space? And what will that be?

My Little Public (MLP) is not a project that criticizes current public space typologies. In fact, the classical definition of public/urban space is still well-recognized and celebrated. MLP is a project that attempts to search for the new potential of future urban spaces in an age where our physical connection is no longer required.

The first initiative of MLP is focused on the numerous vacant lots in downtown Boston. By utilizing these vacant lots, the project attempts

"MLP teaches the next generation to constantly think about what is happening in their environment, and to be aware of the physical spaces they are situated in."

to hold a small-scale, repeated cycle-style contest in searching for the most suitable public program for those lots. With the slogan "In the future, everyone can have his own public space for 30 days," MLP successfully drew attention from a local organization. The Street Lab, an organization that often operates on experimental urban spaces in the Boston area, suggested that the project ought to be first applied to a smaller and more closed network, such as a public school. It might also potentially transform MLP into an educational program to raise awareness among children about the environment they interact with. With this insightful suggestion, MLP found its first real client and testing ground—the Quincy Public School in Boston.

With the help of Philip D. Amara, a fourth grade teacher, we adapted MLP so that the program could operate easily inside the school. This four-week program contained the following steps: first, we introduced three different operation sites to the students, educating them to recognize the nature of the site with the prospect that the proper program be introduced to it; second, we allowed each of the kids to use their own imagination to propose their wishes for the site they chose. During this process, Amara and I were trying not to project too much of our adult thinking onto their proposals. We were amazed by how much the children learned from the previous step, that almost all of their proposals showed advanced understandings of the site, and that they were also highly plausible. More amazingly, some of the proposals not only showed their awareness of the school site but also showed their awareness of current environmental and social issues. During the third week, they selected the six best proposals out of the original 24, and formed official campaign groups for each one. Each group then created a campaign speech. Finally, the winner, Coco-Nade, was carried out during a lunch break—the students sold hot cocoa and lemonade for 50 cents. In total, they raised $110 in 40 minutes, and the profits were donated to a homeless organization.

According to Amara, MLP is perfectly suited to fourth graders, as they are at the age when they can distinguish what is possible from what is not. They can appreciate drafting, editing, and perfecting the work in a methodical process. Most importantly, they are beginning to pay more attention to what is happening around them and attempting to interact with it. MLP made them realize that if they're passionate, they have the power to say or do anything.

In short, MLP doesn't need to go through a governmental process in order to transform an empty lot into a contemporary urban space. MLP can be more successful if it runs in the background of our public education system, which teaches the next generation to constantly think about what is happening in their environment, and to be aware of the physical spaces they are situated in. By educating children while they are young, we can foster their desire to cultivate an engaging and livable environment. It offers the prospect of creating a culture where people have more awareness and interaction with their environment. Hopefully, MLP will become a program that promotes a discussion that could potentially form a new concept of future urban spaces.

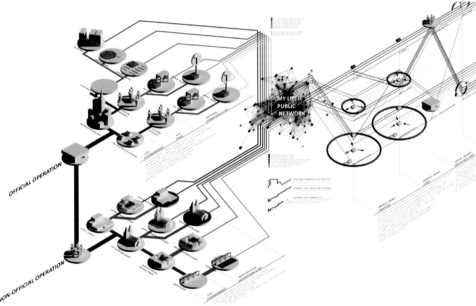

Top: My Little Public at
Quincy School logo

Bottom: Diagram showing the
different scale implementation of
the public network

Right: Pictures of the different
phases of My Little Public being
tested at Quincy School

Dot Future

Kate Balug

Dorchester is a large, historic, and often stigmatized neighborhood in Boston that exhibits diverse elements of urban living. In addition to generations of Irish and Polish Americans, it is home to large Vietnamese, Cape Verdean, and Central and African American populations. Visually, it lacks the New England orderliness prevalent in Boston, and feels more like a chaotic, contemporary global city. My project sought to connect the diverse residents of this neighborhood with ongoing city planning efforts, and amplify their sense of agency over their physical surroundings.

"Radical politics has to begin and end in everyday life, it can't do otherwise. [...] Everyday life is like quantum gravity: by going very small you can perhaps begin to understand the whole structure of life. By changing everyday life you can change the world." —Henri Lefebvre

The implications of a $15-million city planning initiative to improve infrastructure along Dorchester's main corridor, Dorchester Avenue, piqued my interest. Was it paving the way for a developer's dream of gentrification, or could it genuinely improve the quality of life for residents in the contested neighborhoods traversed by the avenue? Through my Networked Urbanism studio project, Dot Future, I sought to first clarify the initiative's intentions to the public, and then generate discussion among a diverse cross-section of the population about how to maximize socioeconomic benefits from this city-designed infrastructure plan. This would finally inform a series of interventions along the street that would operate as a fragmented monument to the past, present, and future of Dorchester. The effort hoped to enhance the sense of community agency over the area's future.

I first studied the proposed changes and community responses to the initiative, and formed a community-based understanding of issues unaddressed by the city's plan. I found

"Let us organize a planning process that enables the important top-down strategies from the city to be complemented by highly place-specific, locally-driven initiatives."

that this area was comprised of many smaller communities that actively promoted their interests, but lacked engagement with politics and with each other across subtle, but firm, community boundaries. Social leaders seldom collaborated with business owners, who in turn remained largely outside of the planning process. Significantly, the concerns of both businesses and residents were perceived as unrelated to the city's commitment to improve infrastructure, so interest in the initiative was minimal.

Embedding myself in the community began awkwardly. I had hoped to learn about the neighborhood by working with youth, but time and again organizations were pleasant but uninterested in collaborating with a student on a yet-to-be-defined project. Pressed by semester deadlines, I approached the *Dorchester Reporter*, a popular local newspaper, with a proposal for a piece. It would describe the planning initiative in plain language and provide updated information about current and upcoming construction. It would include a collaged image of residents' ideas for Dorchester Avenue that took advantage of the improved infrastructure, and invite readers to send in their own.

Once the *Reporter* supported my effort, heads began to shake in a new way. A Main Street organization invited me to lead a community workshop that explored local issues and ways to address them. The Main Street initiative helps local businesses and is intimately connected with the city, representing both public and private interests.

From there I met others who would become significant partners. As the semester finished, I was finally in a place to begin work on a project that would be meaningful to this diverse set of communities and my academic inquiry. My effort continued through thesis research, which focused on place-based collective identity— something I found to be missing and necessary in addressing issues shared across geographic, rather than socially-constructed communities. Then, the project morphed into My Dot Tour,

a multimedia walking tour of Fields Corner, an area along Dorchester Avenue. The tour was led by local youth and featured their commentary on the past, present, and future of Fields Corner. It was developed with several partner organizations and MIT's Center for Civic Media.

The Networked Urbanism studio allowed me to bridge the theoretical understanding acquired at the GSD with the complex, multi-layered nature of urban experience. My goal in Dorchester was to connect spatial experience in an urban environment with social, economic, and public interests, and to employ creative, critical expression as a part of agency-building in everyday life.

Top: My Dot Tour participants   Bottom: Teen tour guides

Top: My Dot community
outreach at the Dorchester Day
Parade to promote the tour

Bottom: "Kite Tales"
story sharing installation

Community (Re)Engagement Project

Irene Figueroa

The project explores the role of design in community empowerment, community engagement, and participatory planning in Villa Victoria. Villa Victoria is a subsidized federal housing project with a large Puerto Rican community located in Boston's South End. It was founded as a result of urban activism by Puerto Ricans and African Americans in the 1960s and 1970s. These collective efforts granted them control over the design of the housing project and its development. The capacity of residents to affect their built environment has been fundamental to maintaining a high level of social capital in the community. During the past few years the community has experienced a series of transformations in the former structures of the community. Even though the residents were affected by these changes, they could not control them. These transformations, combined with lack of power and rumors of a funding shortage, have resulted in fear of displacement. And this fear has translated into a decrease of social capital.

"We were reenacting the origins of the community, which was founded as the result of urban activism."

The studio project aimed to reengage residents with their community through a series of urban planning and design workshops. The workshops allowed residents to publicly discuss urban issues affecting them. After identifying an issue of concern, design and urban activism workshops were created to empower residents to act on concerning problems. Three age groups participated in the workshops and each focused on different problems. At Escuelita Borikén, 4 to 5-year-old students worked on sidewalks and safety. At the Cacique After School Program, 13 to 16-year-old students were interested in addressing urban violence.

During the mapping workshops with the residents, problems of communication were evident. Fear of displacement translated into dialogues with racist overtones, which created problems for any future interventions. An urban activism workshop was planned to address this communication problem, during which we aimed to help them channel their frustration in a positive way.

During the mapping workshop, the youth of Villa Victoria expressed concern about the increase in urban violence. For the design workshop, they designed an urban installation in a park where many crimes have occurred. The workshop served as an opportunity to introduce students to concepts of spatial design. The installation, named Dream Catcher, aimed to transform the park into a positive space and bring awareness to the issue of urban violence. However, the event was cancelled due to snow and severe weather. We plan to install the Dream Catcher next spring.

During the mapping workshop, the students of Escuelita Borikén identified cracks, bumps, and uneven surfaces on the sidewalks of Villa Victoria. For the design workshop, the students painted signs in which they alerted pedestrians about unsafe areas on the ground. Finally, during the urban activism event, the kids went out and placed the signs on the sidewalks of Villa Victoria.

These sessions and small projects served as opportunities to reengage the residents with the urban space and empowered them to act on the issues affecting them. In poetic terms, we were reenacting the origins of the community, which was founded as the result of urban activism.

After seeing the awareness raised by the workshops about how policies and urban systems work, it was evident that these types of exercises can improve and enrich civil society, assuring a better operation of participatory planning processes. The exercise invited residents to think about urban issues, discuss them, and formulate solutions. The whole process allowed them to internalize the issues and engage in critical thinking.

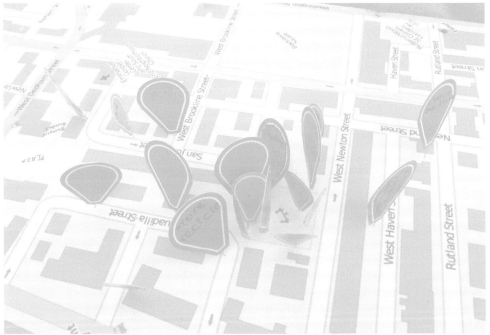

Top: During the mapping workshop, the youth of Villa Victoria expressed concern about the increase in urban violence

Bottom: Students placed markers on a map to highlight issues in their neighborhood

Top: The young students mapping the
cracks on the pathways of Villa Victoria

Bottom: The students painted
signs in which they alert pedestrians
about unsafe areas on the ground

Hear Here!

Joe Liao
Hansley Yuñez

Hear Here! is a location-based discussion board that allows people to connect with each other through the commonality of place. It allows users to engage in threaded discussions that are linked to physical locations. Users can also view discussions in other places by moving their virtual selves to that location. These discussions are persistent—they can be viewed and continued by future users even after the original participants have left. Hear Here! is designed to foster local community and provide an avenue for transient populations to engage with locals and with each other.

Today's highly connected world has enabled new forms of communication that have heretofore been impossible. Platforms such as Facebook, Twitter, and Quora allow us to connect with our friends, followers, or people with shared interests, essentially without regard for their physical location. These new forms of interaction are invaluable in their ability to target a very specific audience in ways that are difficult or impossible without current technologies. But while these technologies have largely erased spatial barriers, their potential for facilitating proximal interactions has been left largely unexplored.

What if there was a platform where we could easily share photos and have discussions with fellow event-goers? What if this platform could let us talk to our neighbors about community news, ask about a lost pet, or put an item up for sale? What if this platform could allow a new tenant to ask existing residents for move-in advice?

Despite the tremendous value in locally-targeted communication, there is as yet no dominant platform through which to do so. Services that connect you with your residential neighborhood do not allow you to engage with

> **"Hear Here! is designed to foster local community and provide an avenue for transient populations to engage with locals and with each other."**

people outside of its boundaries. Those that let people post in predefined public places do not reflect the users' sense of place. And those that allow people to post geolocated messages via their physical location do not capitalize on the inherent advantages of the digital medium to transcend spatial restrictions.

For these reasons we decided to develop our own solution by creating a discussion board that connects people to their own neighborhood or region, creating a sense of place in cyberspace. If a user wishes, they may join discussions in locations other than their own. Just as populations shift and migrate in the real world, users may come and go, leaving one thread to join another, or they may continue to follow threads based in their previous location, in order to maintain contact.

Hear Here! is entirely user generated. Its users create both the content and the geometry of the places to which these topics are tagged. These places can range in scale from a single building to a city district. A place can be as well-defined as a building or as nebulous and transient as an impromptu street festival. And because these places are not defined by top-down categorizations, Hear Here! can provide insight into how people conceive of place.

Hear Here! can be understood as a synthesis of the digital layer with the physical world. Discussions, conversations, and thoughts are mapped to a virtual representation of real space. Hear Here! is still cyberspace—you are free to move your virtual location wherever you want—but it straddles the digital/physical divide in a way that marries the qualities of both kinds of space. It liberates real-world users from physical restrictions by allowing them to engage with others at any place and any time, yet it still retains the real world spatiality that is valuable for targeting users. This spatial duality is still a novel and under-explored conception, but we are excited to see how people utilize it in ways we cannot yet imagine.

This project is now a startup. In 2013 it was selected for further development by the Harvard Innovation Lab, and was a semifinalist for the MIT $100K Entrepreneurship Competition.

YOUR COMMUNITY AT YOUR FINGERTIPS.

Top: Hear Here! logo and concept

Bottom: Your community at your fingertips promo

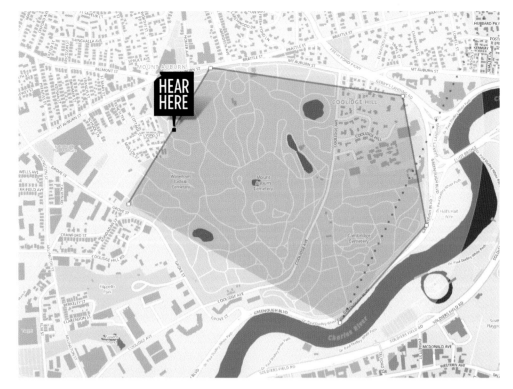

Top: Website map interface   Bottom: Georeferenced locations

Table Talk

Stacy D. Morton

Table Talk is a physical social network connecting
individuals of similar interests by combining the physical
and digital realms of urban space. This new community
typology makes formerly invisible layers of shared interest
visible in material space, connecting individuals in real
time to past occupants.

> **"By embedding personal metadata onto physical objects, a new community workspace is developed, highlighting the importance of the city as place."**

Looking at the history of social networking, social connections first and foremost were always spatial. With the invention of the Internet, social interaction went from physical to digital and new geolocation technology begins to bring the physical back into social networking—yet only as a dot on a map. What if instead of separating our physical and virtual layers there was a way for our physical environment to become a social network?

Table Talk engraves an added layer of digital technology into the static object. Each table is networked into a larger system within the room. As an individual "engraves" their interests onto the table, the system is able to delineate shared layers between occupants and connect users in real time. Once the table receives an individual's interests, it retains that trace so that connections can extend across temporalities. Based on the chance occurrence of choosing the same table, individuals of shared interests can connect through layers of time using the physical environment and adding a heightened importance to place.

With the increased use of the "in-between" place between work and home where individuals come to work independently in public, Table Talk further enhances the social quality of this space. This new typology is a place to work alongside other intellectuals, some of whom may share an inherent knowledge base, and connect on mutually beneficial terms. This type of environment not only provides a workspace, but starts to break social barriers through place, creating a richer way for people to connect, develop community, provide space for organizing, and therefore become a tool for placemaking.

In order for these connections to occur, technology is fully integrated into a responsive LED table in which the physical and digital layers combine. This two-foot by two-foot table prototype is capable of absorbing user interests in two ways. The first is through the display of color in real time. The table is designed using an RGB LED strip embedded at the edge of a maple plywood table topped with frosted acrylic. The tabletop is embedded with a range of topic choices (specific to location). The user simply chooses an interest by touching the engraved surface, and depending on the topic chosen, the table adjusts color. In a room with several of these tables, users can quickly see who else in the room shares a particular interest and connect in real time. The device is also embedded with a further layer of technology allowing the user to connect with past users of that specific table. A QR code for each topic is embedded in the tabletop. When scanned, the user is connected with those who previously happened to choose that exact seat. Users are then able to see notes on that specific topic left from the past and leave further notes for the future.

An installation would feature anywhere from three to five tables; located either within proximity of each other or scattered throughout the exhibit. Users would be encouraged to interact with the table, adjusting its color and connecting to its "memory board." Furthermore, a video of the installation would suggest a deeper connection between users in the space while encouraging social interactions both in real time and to past/future users.

By infiltrating unused spaces with these responsive devices laid out in a way that promotes social interaction, "in-between" space can begin to act as a placemaking tool and means for community engagement. This physical social network can begin to connect individuals on deeper and more meaningful levels depending on their hobby, background, research, or need.

TableTalk

The Physical Social Network

Come. Logon. Talk.

What if there was a way our **physical** environment could become a **social network?**

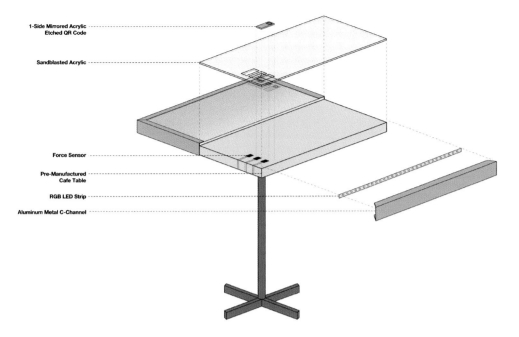

1-Side Mirrored Acrylic Etched QR Code

Sandblasted Acrylic

Force Sensor

Pre-Manufactured Cafe Table

RGB LED Strip

Aluminum Metal C-Channel

Left: Table Talk concept,
the Physical Social Network

Top: Table construction axonometric

Bottom: Table Talk
testing at the GSD café

Corner Stories

Matthew Swaidan

This project began with a question about how people connect to places. As our lives become ever more transient, the stable relationships with place that have defined communities for generations are evaporating. Many of us now inhabit places whose history we have no understanding of and no personal connection to. What happens to the identity of a place when its residents have no memory of it?

Boston has a strong tradition of collecting oral histories of place. Organizations like the Cambridge Historical Commission, South End Historical Society, and other community groups have archived personal stories about people in their neighborhoods, maintaining a link between the physical fabric and the lives it contained. But how many people know about these archives? How many of the current residents can point to a family members' story contained therein? Do these archives invite their viewers to contribute their own stories? Do they encourage us to explore our environment, to connect the physical artifacts with the stories they hold?

Changes in our technological environment have made it easier than ever for us to connect to each other, to share the details of our lives (however banal), and to map with pinpoint precision any number of events. Can these new tools offer an opportunity to bring the archive of personal histories out of the library, onto the street corners where they took place? Rather than simply absorbing our neighbors' stories, shouldn't interactive media allow us to be both speaker and listener? Can we use it to enter a dialogue with the history of a place and to have our own place within that history?

To explore these possibilities, I sought a way to connect personal stories about place with their actual settings. The result was a device that mounts to the nearly ubiquitous street sign. As a person passes by, their curiosity is aroused by a

"What happens to the identity of a place when its residents have no memory of it?"

foreign looking object, inviting them to see what happens when they push the brightly colored button. When she does, she is treated to a highly personal "seed" story, one that takes place on the very ground upon which she stands. "This is where I waited for the bus to school every morning for 11 years of my life. Here I made some of my best friends. I remember the time when…" The viewer is then invited to push the button again, to record their own story about that place, or to react to the story that just played. Over the term of their deployment, the device accrues more and more layers of personal narrative attached to the place.

As I worked on the design, I began to seek content for the device. After meeting with several people who had worked to build oral history archives, I met a group of young high school students who were tackling some of the very same questions as I was. As part of a program called YouthStream, students were learning the art of storytelling, and exploring ways that new visual media allowed them to share their stories. What made the collaboration even more fruitful was that these students were specifically focusing on stories that connected their personal lives with public places: each student picked a street corner in Cambridge that held some personal memory, and developed techniques for conveying that story both visually and orally. By exploring what was happening outside of the walls of the GSD, I was able to find others to work with, which helped me explore my ideas, and allowed me to help them reach a broader audience.

The collaboration resulted in a trial run in January of 2011, which was a moderate success. I installed the device at a bus stop in Union Square, with a seed story about a child's experience of maturation, set at a bus stop and on the bus. The story was funny, touching, poignant, and personal. The device succeeded in attracting listeners, and even recorded a few reactions. Though it didn't work as well as I had hoped, it has led to a new collaboration with another research group at Harvard called metaLab.

While the content has changed in the new exploration, the core idea of connecting people to place through tangible, interactive media remains the focus. What is particularly exciting is that the problem we are working on requires us to explore both the tangible and intangible aspects of media: the physical presence of the object must grab a person's attention, inspire his curiosity, and invite an interaction, while the intangible content must be satisfying, bring joy or a new understanding, and make us think about the world in a way we hadn't before.

Top: The device with the seed story

Bottom: User interacting with the device

Right: Exploded detail of the interactive placemarker

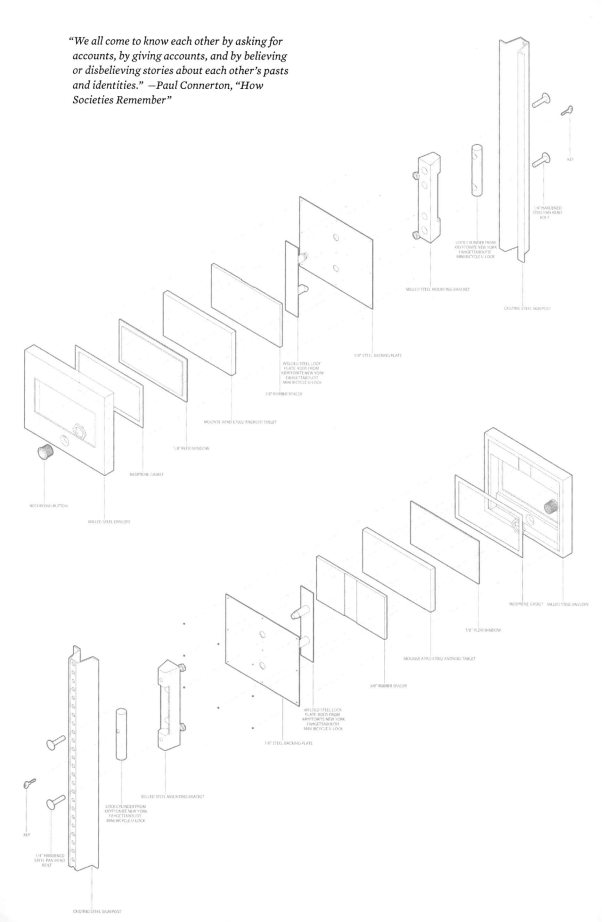

"We all come to know each other by asking for accounts, by giving accounts, and by believing or disbelieving stories about each other's pasts and identities." —Paul Connerton, "How Societies Remember"

1/4" HARDENED STEEL PAN HEAD BOLT

KEY

LOCK CYLINDER FROM KRYPTONITE NEW YORK FAHGETTABOUTIT MINI BICYCLE U-LOCK

MILLED STEEL MOUNTING BRACKET

EXISTING STEEL SIGN POST

1/8" STEEL BACKING PLATE

WELDED STEEL LOCK PLATE; RODS FROM KRYPTONITE NEW YORK FAHGETTABOUTIT MINI BICYCLE U-LOCK

3/8" RUBBER SPACER

MOONSE APAD E7002 ANDROID TABLET

1/8" PLEXI WINDOW

NEOPRENE GASKET

RECORDING BUTTON

MILLED STEEL ENVLOPE

NEOPRENE GASKET   MILLED STEEL ENVLOPE

1/8" PLEXI WINDOW

MOONSE APAD E7002 ANDROID TABLET

3/8" RUBBER SPACER

WELDED STEEL LOCK PLATE; RODS FROM KRYPTONITE NEW YORK FAHGETTABOUTIT MINI BICYCLE U-LOCK

1/8" STEEL BACKING PLATE

MILLED STEEL MOUNTING BRACKET

LOCK CYLINDER FROM KRYPTONITE NEW YORK FAHGETTABOUTIT MINI BICYCLE U-LOCK

KEY

1/4" HARDENED STEEL PAN HEAD BOLT

EXISTING STEEL SIGN POST

MYPS

Jennifer Mills

MYPS is personalized cloud-to-ground cartography that reshapes both how we compose our farewells and how we receive the farewells of others. The app combines the strength of place in the development of memories with the ease of social media sharing formats to make the process of preparing for death and the process of grieving the deaths of others incremental and meaningful.

A P.S. is an afterthought—an easily appended message that crosses our mind after we think we have said all we meant to say. Yet the postscript also contains our final words, which are actually quite powerful. When combined with the power of place in the development of memories, these afterthoughts can create meaningful journeys for our loved ones to revisit after we are gone.

MYPS uses the GPS capabilities of mobile devices in combination with familiar media sharing formats to facilitate authography—the process of authoring and mapping shared memories. Authographers can compose notes, photos, videos, recorded messages, or sketches using the standard built-in features of their mobile device. They will then designate recipients from the list of companions they've included in their account and upload each P.S. to cloud storage using the app. MYPS will organize and georeference each P.S. in order to create maps, which the authographer's companions will receive after the authographer's passing. As the companions follow these journeys, the P.S.es will appear on their device so the companions may literally revisit the memories they shared with the authographer.

Most importantly, MYPS is incremental and connected to real places. Composing a final farewell is as daunting a task as trying to sit down and write a novel from scratch. Authors typically break the work down into manageable

"MYPS reduces the aversion we have to the spaces of death by celebrating the memories of the deceased in the spaces of everyday life."

pieces. However, there is not yet an equivalent approach in the funeral planning industry. MYPS uses familiar and simple media sharing formats such as text messages or tweets, photos or videos captured on phones, and voicemails to make the process of composing farewells incremental. By attaching the media to specific locations, MYPS engages the part of our brain that already geotags our memories. Neurobiologists have recently discovered that the hippocampus attaches locations to memories, accounting for the phenomenon in which a familiar place or scene brings a person back to an experience they may not have thought of in years. The vividness that place brings to memories adds strength to the simple messages stored by MYPS, resulting in journeys that are emotionally powerful yet easier to compose. Moreover, MYPS delivers journeys that can be experienced all at once or gradually, immediately or years after the loved one's passing, making the process of grieving incremental as well.

Over time, MYPS could also tie together multiple generations, as it did when the creator, a young woman living in Boston, interviewed her grandfather, and then took her mother to the places he remembered from his own time living in that city. The mother used MYPS to record the trip so that once she had passed away her daughter could revisit those places again and remember not only her grandfather's stories, but also the time spent together with her mother. Furthermore, if authographers choose to make certain P.S.es public, the accumulation of memories could add a wealth of personal and emotional information to cities that could be valuable to historians, genealogists, tourists, and the like.

MYPS began with an investigation of the waste associated with land used for cemeteries. As infrequently visited, monoprogrammatic places, cemeteries are underutilized. Furthermore, the material waste of casket burials is staggering. While the green burial movement and other proponents of alternative death care have addressed the environmental and emotional concerns arising from this waste, as have

scientists and academics in related fields, their work focuses on the relatively short time span in which a person is dying, being memorialized, or in the immediate stages of grief. Consequently, current solutions do not address people's emotional needs outside of those concentrated moments. MYPS addresses that longer time-span, transforming the process of preparing for death and the process of grieving into positive, shared experiences. In doing so, MYPS reduces the aversion we have to the spaces of death by celebrating the memories of the deceased in the spaces of everyday life. The new ritual will also allow for an updated digital construction of our postmortem identity (just as we digitally curate our living identity with blogs, Pinterest, Facebook, etc.).

Hopefully, MYPS can reduce the waste associated with cemeteries by shifting our perceptions of death and memorialization so that the spaces of death are no longer excluded from the spaces of life.

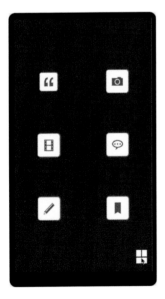

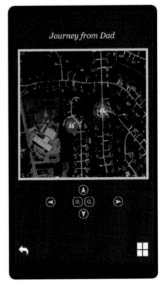

Screenshots from the mobile app
MYPS showing both the record and
the reproduction phase

Screenshots of the video presentation
showing the first field test of the app

The New Statistical Commons

Robert Pietrusko

Public spaces were formerly a venue for debate, where we could collectively imagine the identity and future of communities. In the contemporary moment, the representation of community is often constructed from afar, with little involvement from the public body, in the form of statistics. This project aims to reassert the role of the community in this process by changing the scale and aesthetic of gathering public opinion and demographics.

In the New Statistical Commons, subway turnstiles are playfully turned into an interactive surveying tool, where individuals can pose questions to their neighbors, with real-time feedback, and likewise construct "statistical narratives." We aim to reenergize public space as a venue for collective quantitative introspection. Demographics about the use of public spaces and the opinions of their inhabitants are collected with a real-time visualization system, using the subway turnstiles as a method of voting. However, these otherwise dry statistics are used in a narrative fashion that cause inhabitants to reflect on their condition and their community. These narratives combine the statistics generated at the site with outside, publicly available data feeds to provide a fuller context for the questions being asked and forces acting on the public space in question. The New Statistical Commons is a community-based Web tool that allows anyone to pose a series of questions through the system to the public, create analytical narratives, and ultimately generate reports.

Instead of turnstiles, a set of double doors are used as the survey tool. The installation at the GSD is a simple proof of concept that tests several of the tool's main assumptions on a limited population. The tool generates narratives from simple yes-or-no questions, draws in additional data feeds for richer stories and lets the student body pose questions to their peers through an e-mail interface—ultimately receiving their results back in the form of a simple report.

no.

19

yes.

14

66.7 % of you probably
need more sleep

Since then the majority of
you are feeling pretty bad

67%

33%

dA?

081

53.3%

dA?

46.7%

071

Above: The prototype installed
at the GSD entrance

Right: Spatial sequencing
at subway stations

2ND ORDER

2ND ORDER

section   plan

Bikenapped

Bikenapped is an online platform aimed at raising awareness and mapping bike thefts in Boston. For the public, Bikenapped serves as a place to get a clearer picture of the bike theft problem as well as a community where users can share experiences. Bikenapped aims to raise awareness for bike thefts and empower cyclists to take action.

As Boston works toward becoming a world-class bicycling city, promotion of cycling and cycling infrastructure has resulted in a significantly growing ridership. However, this increase in cycling correlates with another phenomenon: the dramatic increase in bicycle thefts.

Bike theft is notoriously difficult to investigate, and stolen bicycles are equally difficult to recover. Theft victims often feel violated and helpless in the face of these crimes. There is nowhere for them to speak out, no outlet for them to take action. By gathering this community of individual voices, we can speak as a collective to shed light on the problem, and work together to find solutions.

One of the issues regarding bike theft lies in the shortage of data on these crimes. According to the reports from the Department of Justice, for every bike theft that is reported to the police, four or more thefts may have occurred. This severe underreporting prohibits us from seeing the full scope of the problem and from allocating adequate resources to tackle it. Bikenapped asks the community to participate in a user-generated mapping of theft incidents, to share information with our neighbors and our city.

Raising awareness and disseminating information is crucial in addressing bike thefts. We seek to take the data beyond the digital realm and into the urban environment we live in. Bike-

...napped asks users to post notices at the physical site of the theft to warn others of what happened. The information is not relevant on the Internet alone; it is relevant to everyone who uses the spaces where these thefts happen.

Change happens when we empower everyone to act. While bike theft is something most people experience alone, Bikenapped seeks to connect us with our neighbors and community. If we discover that other people have had their bikes stolen from the same place as ours, perhaps we can join together to demand for better safety measures in our neighborhood. If law enforcement is aware of certain zones of bike thefts, perhaps they are better equipped to police the area. If we know bikes have been stolen from a particular place, perhaps we will all be more vigilant to keep our neighborhoods safe from bike theft.

The project began with data collection. Through visiting police departments and combing through public log information, we can already begin to see the difficulty in just understanding the bike theft issue in Cambridge. In the city of Cambridge alone, there are three separate police departments that hold jurisdiction over different areas: the Cambridge Police Department, the Harvard University Police Department, and the MIT Police Department. In addition, the MBTA Transit Police oversees all transit stops. All of these police departments have separate reporting and record keeping methods, which are not collated into a single database, but rather are organized internally. From any one source, we can only see a narrow segment of the larger problem. It became clear that in order to understand the issue, we needed a place where information can be collated and made accessible to the public.

Bikenapped became a platform to not merely disseminate information, but also encourage participation. Bike thefts are severely underreported due to the common perception that nothing will come from a police report. Though the rates of recovery are surely low—and

Bikenapped makes no claims at increasing the chances of recovery—a report on Bikenapped is something theft victims see. It is visible on the map, and visible to every person who comes to visit it. A piece of information, or an experience where a victim had once suffered alone, is now directly and visibly making a contribution to a larger story and effort.

The reaction to Bikenapped has been extremely positive. As different media outlets and cycling blogs began to pick up the story, reports and e-mails started coming in. We had over 2,500 unique visitors within the first 12 days, many from beyond the borders of Boston/Cambridge, all the way from Portland and California. The issue surely struck a chord with people, and the support and response that Bikenapped received validated the need for its existence.

Since it launched, bikenapped.com has been featured in Metro.us and BostInno, as well as several bicycling-specific blogs and websites.

Report a Bikenapping

(1) Fill out the form

name

email

date of incident

time of incident

bike description

value

set up

lock type

tell your story

photo url

PLACE MARKER

(2) Tag the city

PRINT and post the flyer where
your bike went missing.

Top: Form to report a "bikenapping"

Bottom: Flyer showing date
and location of a theft

Right: General view of the map
with all theft reports in Cambridge

BIKENAPPED!

Bikenapped: Harvard student creates website to track bicycle thefts

After Harvard graduate student Lulu Li had not one, but two of her beloved bicycles stolen, she decided to take action.

A little over a week ago, the 25-year-old design student launched Bikenapped.com, a website that allows cyclists to map the locations of bicycle thefts and share their stories. Scorned cyclists can also print a "Bikenapped" flyer to post at the location of the theft, warning other riders to take precautions.

Top: The reaction to Bikenapped has been extremely positive, different media like *Metro.us* and *BostInno* began to pick up the story

Bottom: A flyer posted where a bike went missing

Right: Data and statistics of bike thefts

Bike Thefts by Month
Source: Harvard Police Department (2005-2012)

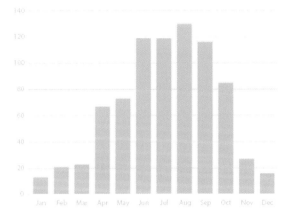

6 years of public log data shows a clear pattern of theft. Bike thefts are much more prevelant in the summer months than over winter. This may correlate with the decrease in ridership and fewer bikes on the streets during the winter.

Thefts by Lock Type
Source: Harvard Police Department (2011)

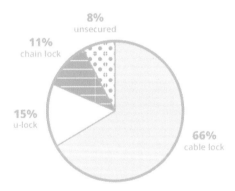

Majority of bikes stolen were locked with cable locks. Cable locks can be easily compromised by common tools found at hardware stores and provide little deterrent for thieves. Unsecured bikes were stolen in residential areas, left on porches or yards. While u-locks are not foolproof, they are more effective at preventing theft.

Costs
Source: Harvard Police Department (2012)

$497
average property loss per theft

From the public police logs, the value of bikes lost ranges from $50-$3000. This averages to just under $500 per bike stolen. With 473 reports currently on bikenapped, this amounts to over $235,000 in reported property loss this year. (This figure is constantly updating as more reports are made.)

Place Pixel

Scott Liang
Thomas McCourt
Benjamin Scheerbarth

Place Pixel is a Web-based application that enables the public to explore the city in entirely new ways. Through the collection and mapping of real-time public sentiment, Place Pixel also generates a layer of information that can provide planners and policy-makers with profound insights into how people experience the city.

Physical planning and urban design decisions are increasingly guided by the patterns expressed through massive amounts of networked data. As a driving force, the smart city paradigm seeks to revolutionize the way we collect, quantify, and analyze this data, allowing for a depth of insight and degree of responsiveness that would have seemed impossible just a few years ago. Preoccupation with objective information, however, will yield models that are inadequate representations of the true urban condition—a condition largely defined by what one might call the first two meters of a city, the human layer. In order to achieve the next level of fidelity, a social variation on the smart city must incorporate the systematic collection and analysis of subjective impressions and emotive responses to the built environment. The need for subjectivity in imaging the city was a concept the Situationists explored a half-century ago. The radical group of French artists, intellectuals, and political theorists engaged in the practice of *dérive*, drifting through the city based on intuition and affection. What happens if, using smart city technologies such as locative media and real-time data sourcing, we ask this very simple question on a larger scale: How do we feel in a space? Essentially, do we like it?

This is exactly the question that the Web-based application Place Pixel explores. At its core lies a seamless interface that allows its users to effortlessly express like or dislike of a space, or a subjective experience in space. The entire city is divided into a georeferenced digital grid,

> **"A social variation on the smart city must incorporate the systematic collection and analysis of subjective impressions and emotive responses to the built environment."**

where each cell, or pixel, takes votes at the push of a button. The application will then render the aggregated layer of likeability in a form that is thoroughly compatible with the wealth of objective information that smart cities already collect.

The key difference to other civic engagement apps lies in the idea of collecting data on the back-end of an app that users engage because they believe it delivers a value greater than the collective construction of a likeability layer. In order to encourage continuous input and a dedicated user base, Place Pixel's interface is designed as an attractive, useable, and rewarding social networking platform that could be used every day to connect to other people and explore the city. Users can see real-time urban conditions around them, from popular places to more ephemeral phenomena such as festivals or demonstrations. Through following thematic pioneers, one can chase street art, dog-friendly places downtown, specialty shopping, or create a follower base oneself.

The resulting network of subjective data is tied to real time and real space. Once overlaid with objective data such as weather, air quality, transportation networks, or noise levels, the result will be much more than a representational exercise, although it surely transforms the way we view our cities, too. Planners and designers can explore the complex systems of interactions within the city in entirely new ways, gaining unprecedented insight into what really creates the "good" in a city.

Place Pixel has been in development for several months, and the process has drawn on the input of numerous researchers and experts in a variety of fields at the intersection of design, technology, and urbanism. The concept for Place Pixel began as part of the Networked Urbanism studio at the GSD, but quickly gained wider attention. The technical approach was refined through discussions with researchers and student groups at the MIT and the MIT SENSEable City Lab. Contributions from researchers at Northeastern University—experts in the study of

social networks and distributed systems analysis—helped to identify some of the shortcomings in other contemporary attempts to generate, collect, and map subjective information. Place Pixel was the basis for a winning proposal in an urban design competition at ABX2013, New England's largest architecture and building-industry conference. With requests to pilot the application from the Mayor's Office of New Urban Mechanics in both Boston and Philadelphia, as well as a network of support from researchers at some of North America's premier academic institutions, Place Pixel has the potential to play a promising role in our evolving methods of studying, visualizing, and experiencing the urban environment.

In 2014 Place Pixel has undergone further development through several competitions and collaborative efforts at the Harvard Innovation Lab, including the 2013 Harvard President's Challenge for innovative approaches to efficient governance, and has become a startup company.

PLACE**PIXEL**

 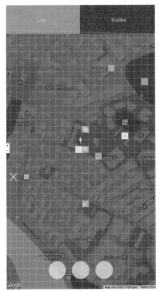 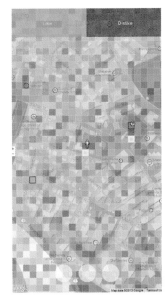

Top: Place Pixel interface showing the login screen (left), the personal map through the "Drift" function (middle) and the community-generated map of the "Here" function (right)

Bottom: The app in use

Right: Part of the app wireframe diagram

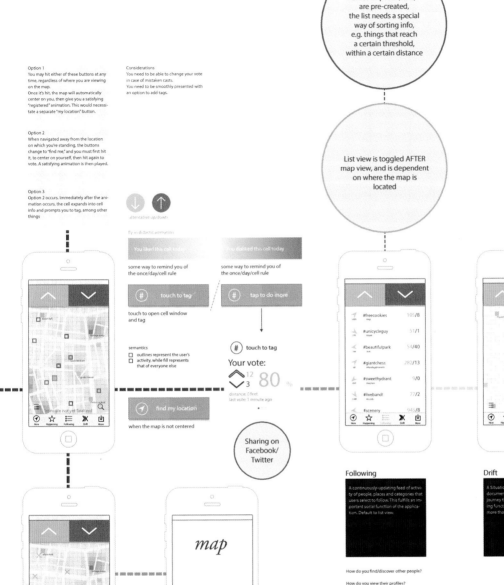

Option 1
You may hit either of these buttons at any time, regardless of where you're viewing on the map.
Once it's hit, the map will automatically center on you, then give you a satisfying "registered" animation. This would necessitate a separate "my location" button.

Option 2
When navigated away from the location on which you're standing, the buttons change to "find me," and you must first hit it, to center on yourself, then hit again to vote. A satisfying animation is then played.

Option 3
Option 2 occurs. Immediately after the animation occurs, the cell expands into cell info and prompts you to tag, among other things

Considerations
You need to be able to change your vote in case of mistaken casts.
You need to be smoothly presented with an option to add tags.

Since all posts (cells) are pre-created, the list needs a special way of sorting info, e.g. things that reach a certain threshold, within a certain distance

List view is toggled AFTER map view, and is dependent on where the map is located

alternative up/down

fly in didactic animation

You liked this cell today

some way to remind you of the once/day/cell rule

You disliked this cell today

some way to remind you of the once/day/cell rule

touch to tag

touch to open cell window and tag

tap to do more

semantics
☐ outlines represent the user's activity, while fill represents that of everyone else

touch to tag

Your vote:
12
3   80 %
distance: 0 feet
last vote: 1 minute ago

find my location

when the map is not centered

Sharing on Facebook/ Twitter

#freecookies   105/8
#unicycleguy   51/1
#beautifulpark   54/40
#giantchess   282/13
#sweethydrant   9/0
#liveband!   77/2
#scenery   945/8

Here Happening Following Drift More

Here Happening Following Drift More

Following
A continuously-updating feed of activity of people, places and categories that users select to follow. This fulfills an important social function of the application. Default to list view.

Drift
A Situationist-inspired blank canvas for documenting one's own emotional journey through a city. A very intriguing function that we intend to explore more thoroughly.

How do you find/discover other people?

How do you view their profiles?

Can you follow cells? Bookmarks?

Follow tags (within a distance)

map

Q Search

Q W E R T Y U I O P
A S D F G H J K L
Z X C V B N M

Satisfying visual confimation of "vote" cast

Pioneers, Celebrities, Explorers

Guest users?

More
Where other important functions are embedded, such as view one's own profile, changing settings and accessing statistics.

HOW IT WORKS:

In *Pixel*, the world is divided into a grid of small, house-sized cells—or pixels.

As the user navigates the city, *Pixel* uses the geolocation technology in her mobile device to sense which pixel she occupies.

GPS

When she encounters anything that resonates with her, she can record her experience by simply tapping:

 like

-or-

 dislike

Then, she can add additional qualitative data such as a:

 comment

-or-

 image

Pixel then does the work for her:

Presenting her with a map of her experiences in space, visualizing her input in aggregate with other users, and allowing her to easily follow and share with people she cares about.

Top: Project flyer

Bottom: City-level visualization

Right: GSD Gund Hall model showing overlapping layers of "likeability"

AEON

Angela Clubb
Khyati Saraf

AEON is a time-balancing tool for a new era. Holistic, visually inspiring, and privileging flexibility over linearity, AEON innovatively combines the calendar and to-do list, and helps find time for the important things in life. With a basis in neuroscience, AEON's qualitative approach facilitates efficacy and integrates space for restorative moments.

Time—there never seems to be enough of it. Even as technology increases our efficiency, we continue rushing, often leading to imbalance and ineffectiveness in our lives. As we strive for productivity, we often underrate the critical role of rest in our cognitive and creative abilities. Multitasking has become the norm, diminishing our capacity to focus on one task at a time. Perhaps most of all, in the rush to complete everything on our plate, we often put off the important things in life. Combined, these imbalances lead to wasted time in our lives.

Time wasted includes what we do with our time and how we do it. But it also includes how we look at it. Our approach to time as a society is indicative of how we perceive it. Our perception and approach translate not only to our relative effectiveness in how we use time but also to our sense of time, such as a feeling of satisfaction and wholeness, or lack thereof. AEON is both a reaction and answer to modern civilization's perception of time and deeply embedded roots in a mechanized approach. It is born out of both the frustration of time wasted as well as the celebration of time itself.

AEON was created to be a time-balancing tool for a new era: a revisualization of time that could help us approach time better. With a vision to create a smarter, flexible, holistic time-balancing tool, the project responds to

> "AEON is both a reaction and answer to modern civilization's perception of time and deeply embedded roots in a mechanized approach."

the limitations of current time-management instruments, which are linear, rigid, and future-oriented; emphasize quantity over quality; and fail to account for importance or integrate the unscheduled.

AEON's design lies at the cusp of a host of scientific and philosophical discourses. Its holistic revisualization conveys a sense of time as whole and present versus linear and constantly passing us by. The tool employs complementary functions and design principles: alternating periods of focus and rest; emphasizing the present and reflecting on the past. Working in tandem, these features not only facilitate a more effective approach to time, their juxtapositions also allow a sense of fulfillment in time well spent.

AEON consists of four functions: Day + Meta (under the category of Time), and Space + Focus.

Day + Meta

Day and Meta are complementary portions of the tool that emphasize a focus on the present and reflection on the past, respectively. The Day view radically revisualizes time to encompass both scheduled and unscheduled activities in a holistic, 24-hour-day view oriented to the present. Scheduled activities appear along the circumference of the day, while unscheduled activities related to our important to-dos appear in the middle and can be flexibly scheduled by dragging to the perimeter. AEON further assists in completing these to-dos by recognizing opportunity and identifying potential gaps in our day. Meanwhile, Meta is the reflective part of the tool. It can track designated activities, such as important to-dos like "Call mom." This function serves to reveal past patterns and activity to increase self awareness and inform better decisions.

Space + Focus

Space and Focus are dichotomous functions that emphasize downtime and intense periods of concentration, respectively, to allow for balance and effectiveness. Research shows that the subconscious network responsible for creativity, learning, and problem solving is strengthened during downtime. The Space function in AEON elevates downtime to its rightful position as a vital component of our effective functioning. It integrates downtime throughout the day and can facilitate cognitive rest through an audio sensory experience. On the flip side, studies show that to perform effectively, our mind needs to focus on one task at a time. AEON supports sustained attention by facilitating a disruption-free environment where e-mail, chat, and calls can be blocked.

Through these various functions, AEON supports users in approaching time more effectively and accomplishing what's important to them, conveying a sense of time as a whole. It facilitates a new, balanced approach that transforms wasted time.

This project was shortlisted as a semifinalist for the 2013 Harvard Business School Pitch competition.

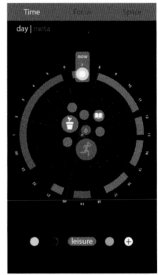

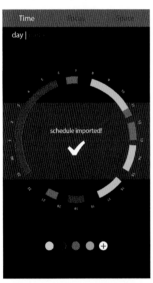

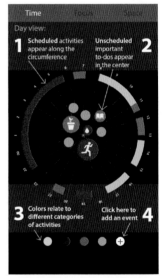

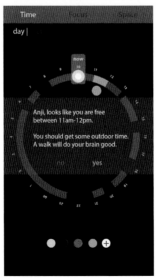

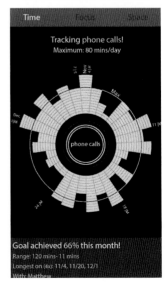

Angela Clubb + Khyati Saraf

Introduction: Focus

aeon recognizes when you have a specific task to complete.

Introduction: Focus

It then facilitates a disruption-free environment to help you focus.

now
11   12   13

You have a report to write now!

Time to focus!

disruption-free zone

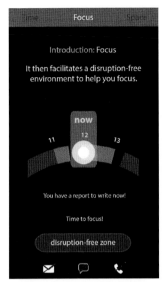

Introduction: Focus

aeon allows you to set a timer for your chosen period of focus.

00:20:00

disruption-free zone

Introduction: Space

Research shows that to be effective, we need to both

Focus   +   Rest

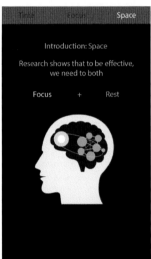

Introduction: Space

The blue bubbles in your day view are downtime which can be scheduled by dragging to the perimeter.

aeon also suggests when you can take downtime during a gap in your schedule.

Introduction: Space

The space timer can facilitate cognitive downtime through an audio sensory experience which is scientifically proven to induce a meditative state.

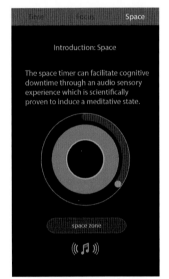

space zone

(((♫)))

You should call mom!
Not meeting input frequency - 2x week

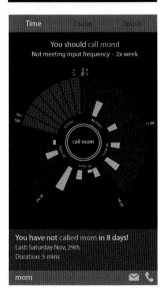

call mom

You have not called mom in 8 days!
Last: Saturday Nov, 29th
Duration: 5 mins

mom

day | meta

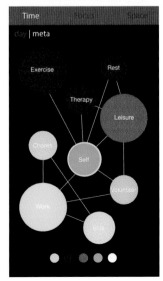

Exercise   Rest
Therapy
Leisure
Chores
Self
Volunteer
Work
Bills

day | meta

Instagraming   Friends
Dog Walking
Sailing   Me time
Studio   Chilling
TV   Space
Walks   Work   Sleep   cooking
Call Mom   Bills
Family
laundry   Newsletter   Shopping
meditate

Contributors

Belinda Tato and Jose Luis Vallejo
are both Design Critics in Urban Planning
and Design at the GSD. Since 2010 they
have been the Networked Urbanism
studio instructors at the GSD, where they
launched an innovative academic approach
to contemporary urbanism, blending design
thinking with social entrepreneurship. They
were recently appointed 2014 Distinguished
Visiting Professors of Urbanism at Portland
State University and are teaching the Design
& Technology Lab at IE University. Tato and
Vallejo are founding members of Ecosistema
Urbano, a Madrid-based group of architects
and urban designers operating within the fields
of urbanism, architecture, engineering, and
sociology that has designed and implemented
projects in multiple countries. They describe
their approach as "urban social design,"
focusing on the design of environments, space,
and dynamics as a way of improving self-
organization among citizens, social interaction
within communities, and their relationship with
the environment.

Paul B. Bottino
established Harvard University's undergraduate
programs in innovation and entrepreneurship
in 2000 with the founding of the Technology
and Entrepreneurship Center at Harvard
(TECH) where he serves as executive director
and lecturer. Bottino is an award-winning
teacher and course designer who has created,
collaborated on, and delivered experiential
education since 2001, including: Innovation
in Science and Engineering; Biotechnology
Startup: Public, Private and Global Health
Ventures; Idea Translation: Effecting Change
through the Arts and Sciences; Social
Entrepreneurship; and Startup R&D. Bottino's
advisory work with over 300 teams of student-
innovators is at every stage of development
and in diverse sectors, including hardware,
software, medical devices, consumer Internet,
global health, energy, social services, and
education.

Blair Kamin
has been the *Chicago Tribune*'s architecture
critic since 1992. A graduate of Amherst
College and the Yale School of Architecture,
he has also been a fellow at the Nieman
Foundation for Journalism at Harvard
University. The University of Chicago Press
has published two collections of Kamin's
columns: *Why Architecture Matters: Lessons
from Chicago* (2001) and *Terror and Wonder:
Architecture in a Tumultuous Age* (2010).
Kamin is the recipient of 35 awards, including
the Pulitzer Prize for Criticism, which he
received in 1999 for a body of work highlighted
by a series of articles about the problems and
promise of Chicago's greatest public space, its
lakefront.

Lulu Li
studied architecture as an undergraduate at Yale University, before completing her MArch I at the GSD in 2014. She was a 2012 Networked Urbanism studio participant. Interested in the intersection of design and technology, Li has explored projects in alternative digital media including Web and video games. Her work—including Bikenapped—has been featured in various media publications including *Boston Magazine*, *Boston Metro*, and *BostInno*.

Scott Liang
is the biggest design geek on the planet. A student of the GSD, he has a background in both architecture and landscape architecture, and has recently developed a deep passion for UX design. Liang also loves getting involved: as a Peace Corps Volunteer in South Africa, he put together English, life skills, and computer literacy programs while assisting HIV/AIDS efforts. Here at home, he's served in various positions in both student and city governments.

Thomas McCourt
is a man of many passions and diverse interests. After studying literature and creative writing in college, McCourt became a published poet. He transitioned away from fine arts to begin law school, where he concentrated in environmental and land-use law. After graduating with a JD, he enrolled in the Master of Urban Planning program at the GSD. There, he combined a life-long love of maps, cities, and people with a practical education in urban governance.

Benjamin Scheerbarth
is a student of Urban Planning at the GSD. His academic interests include international planning, strategic urban design, and smart cities. His background is in organizational studies, which he studied in Manchester and Copenhagen. In his professional future, Scheerbarth aims to explore the impact of cross-cultural contingencies on planning processes. He remains convinced that a strong understanding of planning interventions is an underexplored dimension of sustainability in contemporary planning practice.

Colophon

Networked Urbanism
Instructors
Belinda Tato, Jose Luis Vallejo
Report Editors
Belinda Tato, Jose Luis Vallejo
Report Design
Enrique Agudo, Molly Huang, Carlos Leon,
Hung Kai Liao, Marco Rizzetto, Rachel Weston

A Harvard University Graduate
School of Design Publication
**Dean and Alexander and Victoria
Wiley Professor of Design**
Mohsen Mostafavi
Assistant Dean for Communications
Benjamin Prosky
Editor in Chief
Jennifer Sigler
Senior Editor
Melissa Vaughn
Associate Editor
Leah Whitman-Salkin
Publications Coordinator
Meghan Sandberg

Series design by Laura Grey and Zak Jensen

ISBN 978-1-934510-39-1

Acknowledgments
Special thanks to Rahul Mehrotra, Chair of the
Department of Urban Planning and Design,
for his continued support and for making this
publication possible.

Image Credits
All courtesy of Marco Rizzetto, except:
Cover: Flickr user Maik, flic.kr/p/bUzrKw; CC
by 2.0
Page 17: Scott Liang, Thomas McCourt,
Benjamin Scheerbarth
Page 24–25: Based on a photograph by Flickr
user Richard Schneider, flic.kr/p/n7Q2av; CC
by NC 2.0
Page 84–85: Carlos Leon

The editors have attempted to acknowledge all
sources of images used and apologize for any
errors or omissions.

Harvard University
Graduate School of Design
48 Quincy Street
Cambridge, MA 02138

publications@gsd.harvard.edu
gsd.harvard.edu